An unsere guten
Freunde Anni + Willi
von Karli + Julia
Okt 18. 98.

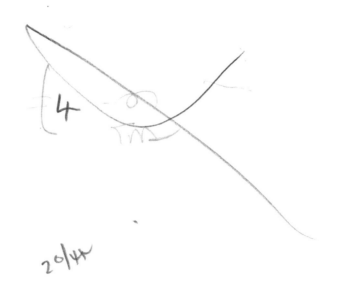

4

20/44

AN ILLUSTRATED HISTORY
of the
HUDSON'S BAY COMPANY

PRO PELLE CUTEM

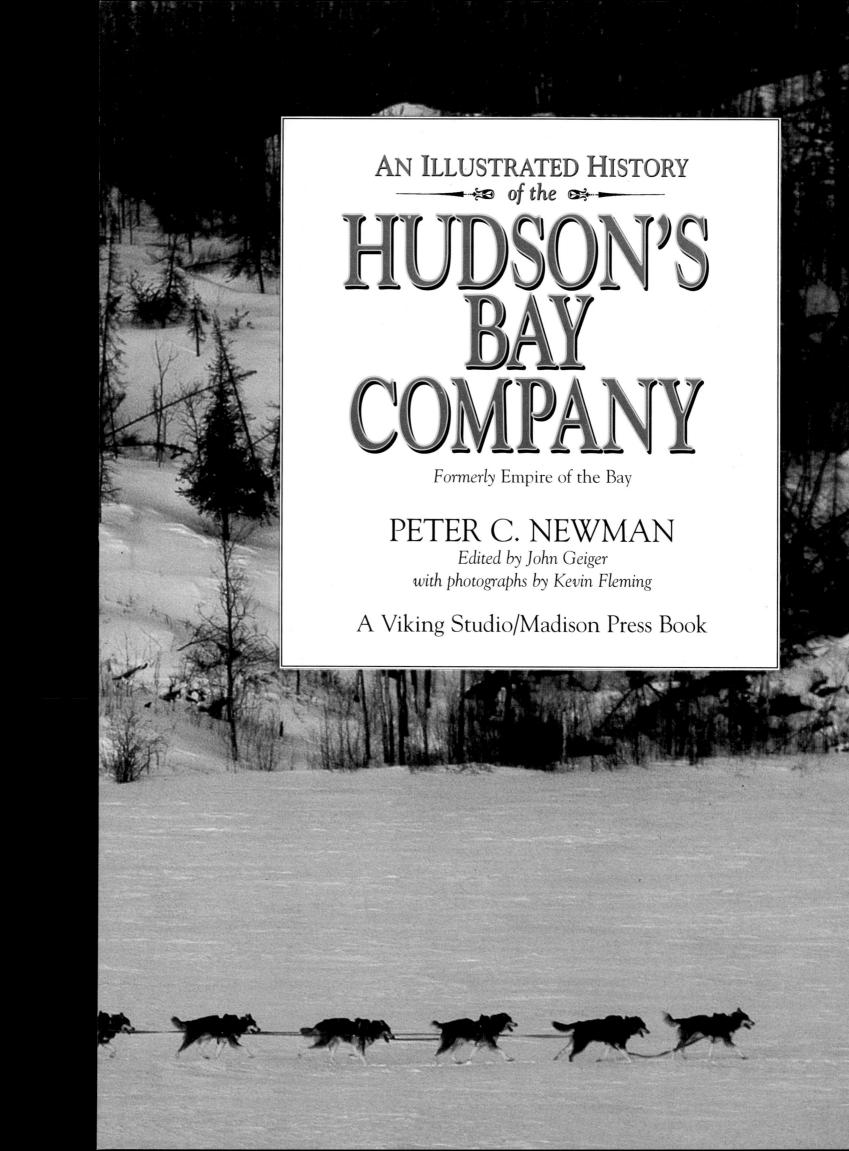

AN ILLUSTRATED HISTORY
of the
HUDSON'S BAY COMPANY

Formerly Empire of the Bay

PETER C. NEWMAN

Edited by John Geiger
with photographs by Kevin Fleming

A Viking Studio/Madison Press Book

*(Endpapers) A detail from an eighteenth
century etching depicting the industrious beavers
of North America building their dams.*

Viking Studio Books

Published by
Penguin Books Canada Ltd,
10 Alcorn Avenue, Suite 300,
Toronto, Ontario
M4V 3B2

First published in 1989 as *Empire of the Bay*

Canadian Cataloguing in Publication Data

CIP data available on request

ISBN 0-670-86534-6

**Produced by
Madison Press Books**
40 Madison Avenue
Toronto, Ontario
M5R 2S1

Printed in Italy

CONTENTS

To the memory of my friend
and mentor, H. Albert Hochbaum,
the most sensitive and perceptive
of the Arctic explorers.

PROLOGUE

THE VACANT WINDOWS OF THE NOW-empty "Big House" catch the dying rays of a far-north sunset. On an adjoining building a stray mongrel absorbs the radiant warmth from the rooftop....

This is York Factory. Once the Hudson's Bay Company's great tidewater headquarters, it now stands abandoned on the shores of the Hayes River. Every so often native trappers wander by, singing as they pass to ward off the evil spirits they believe inhabit the huge white building. Now and again a polar bear pads around the sacred confines of the depot's courtyard, searching for meat and companionship.

For 249 years the Hudson's Bay Company sent tall-masted supply ships from its docks in London to an anchorage seven miles offshore from here called Five Fathom Hole. While these majestic vessels rode gently on their anchor chains, sloops sent out from the Factory ferried ashore cargoes of guns, brandy, textiles, knives, axes and other trade goods. The vacated holds were then filled with bundles of furs brought to York Factory from the trading posts strung out over the three million square miles of the Company's empire. From Fort Garry and Fort Edmonton fifteen hundred miles away, first the canoe brigades and then flotillas of flat-bottomed York boats traversed a continent's waterways bearing a winter's harvest of furs to within site of the hexagonal cupola of the main depot building.

For generations York Factory was not only a major centre of North American commerce but also the point of entry for those who chose to enlist in the Company's service. To the raw recruits brought out to man the HBC's forts and trading posts, as well as the missionaries, botanists, geologists, Arctic explorers (including Sir John Franklin), and later, the settlers and troops who defended them — the great white complex on the barren shore provided their first impression of a new world.

Here the history and present-day reality of the Hudson's Bay Company come together. Once the hub of a vast commercial empire, the old post declined with the advent of railroads and finally closed its doors in 1957. For more than three centuries the Company has shuttled between splendour and dust, unstoppable momentum and impending collapse. Today York Factory stands as an apt example of the Hudson's Bay Company's extraordinary ability to slough off the past and expediently renew itself in other places, other guises.

LA CACCIA DEI CASTORI.

CHAPTER ONE

A KINGDOM BY ITSELF

"THE HUDSON'S BAY IS NOT AN ORDINARY COMMERCIAL company, but a kind of kingdom by itself, and it needs statesmen to administer it," the novelist John Buchan once observed. Although suitable statesmen have seldom been found at its helm, John Buchan (who as First Baron Tweedsmuir was Governor General of Canada during the late 1930s) was quite correct. The Hudson's Bay Company has indeed functioned as a kingdom for well over three hundred years.

During the first two centuries of its existence, the span of this kingdom was outlined by a network of trading posts that reached from the Arctic Ocean to Hawaii, and as far south as San Francisco. Founded in Restoration England to supply the demands of fashion for beaver hats, the Company soon grew into a fur-trading colossus. At the peak of its expansion it controlled nearly three million square miles of territory – nearly a twelfth of the earth's land surface and an area ten times that of the Holy Roman Empire at its height.

The oldest continuous commercial enterprise still in existence, the Company has weathered 319 years of war, rebellion, ambush, siege, bumbling bureaucracy and coupon-clipping neglect. Despite financial losses in recent years, it remains a major economic force as Canada's largest department store chain, and as a significant international player in real estate, stuffing nearly five billion Canadian dollars into its revenue coffers in 1988. It has survived the trials of the centuries by turning nearly every necessity into an opportunity, and by never moving too fast. Although to its detractors the initials HBC have stood for "the Hungry Belly Company" or "the Horny Boys Club," the motto of the Bay men who bent their efforts to producing maximum profits should have been "Wait and Seize."

York Factory, located in northern Manitoba on the shores of Hudson Bay, could stand as a symbol for the Company. This is where the Company first perfected the fur trade as a world-scale

(Opposite) A 1777 European engraving portrays beavers living in condominium-style colonies.

enterprise. Established in 1684, it was from here that most of its pathfinders set off to probe its inland empire.

Long the North American headquarters for the Hudson's Bay Company, the great seaboard fort fell into disuse in this century. The Cree, whose ancestors had been trading there for two hundred years, came in ever-diminishing numbers and, in 1957, York Factory was abandoned. Most of its buildings were pulled down or ravaged by vandals. Although its great white depot building remains standing, York Factory today is little more than a haunted memorial to the HBC's involvement in the fur trade. Conditions changed and the Company changed with them, without a backward glance.

If the Hudson's Bay Company prospered by its shrewdness and guile, it was born out of a sort of romance – the passionate union of *Castor canadensis* and European fashion. Today's fancier of mink or Persian lamb might find it hard to believe, but beaver was once considered the world's most valuable fur. Before the invention of the umbrella, beaver headgear provided an elegant way to keep dry. There was much more to the fashion than mere practicality, however. Men and women could be instantly placed within the social hierarchy according to their hats, and, as American historian Walter O'Meara wrote, "To own a fine beaver was to prove one's standing as a man – or woman – of the beau monde." So valuable were beaver pelts that the sand from the floor in warehouses where they were stored was sifted to salvage every last hair. By 1854, when the fashion in beaver hats had already passed its heyday, 509,000 pelts had been auctioned off in London alone.

When Charles II awarded "the Company of Adventurers" a charter in 1670 as "true Lordes and Proprietors" of all the sea and lands of Hudson Bay and its entire drainage system, the boundaries of that empire were not fixed by charter so much as by the habits of that pug-nosed rodent with the lustrous coat.

It was the beavers themselves, peering myopically from the portcullises of their mud and twig castles, that led the interlopers ever deeper into North America's hinterland. The beaver is a non-migratory animal that needs relatively large spaces to live in, so that once a creek was "beavered out" hunters had to move on, deeper and farther into the New Land. Just as the stalking of elephants for their tusks lured white hunters into the heart of Africa, so the pelts of the beaver drew traders from both Hudson Bay and the St Lawrence towards the snow-capped Rocky Mountains and eventually to the vast Pacific.

The Company's travellers were aided in their hunt for furs by geography. By choosing to settle the deserted shores of Hudson

An eighteenth-century artist's impression of a beaver.

A fur-trade canoe shooting the rapids.

Bay rather than more attractive landfalls to the south, the early traders appropriated the overwhelming advantage of being able to deliver their trade goods into the very heart of the new continent, for the network of wide rivers that flowed to Hudson Bay rolled through a fur-rich hinterland stretching back to the foothills of the Rocky Mountains. Another advantage that allowed the fur trade to flourish was that most of Canada's huge drainage system is interconnected by relatively short portages. With few impediments, it is possible to cross the upper half of the continent east of the Rockies by canoe.

The Company's importance in the formation of Canada is largely a result of this tenuous occupation. The presence of HBC traders kept the Canadian West out of the grasp of American colonizers pushing northward. The 1870 sale of Company territory to the new nation of Canada let the former colonies fill in their northern and western boundaries, and three of the early HBC trading posts – Fort Garry (now Winnipeg), Fort Edmonton and Fort Victoria – grew into provincial capitals. Company officers charted the Arctic coast and mapped much of Canada's West, including the rugged interior of British Columbia. The Company's self-proclaimed gentleman adventurers virtually created Canada, but notions that the HBC might be destined for such lofty purposes as discovering the North West Passage, colonizing the New World or "converting the savages" were always summarily dismissed by its Governors. The HBC was much more interested in making profit than making history.

This single-minded drive for greater revenues coloured everything the Company did. For its first two centuries, the HBC was dedicated to maintaining its vaunted fur trade monopoly established by the regal trio who were its first governors – Prince Rupert, the Duke of York and the Duke of Marlborough. Threatened by fleets of French warships in the early days, the greatest peril to the

HBC came later, from a rival fur-trading enterprise, the North West Company. Like crusaders of the Middle Ages, the Nor'Westers ultimately failed in their quest and trampled the banner under which they set out to conquer a continent. But for almost four decades, from 1783 to 1820, the Montreal-based North West Company challenged the power and majesty – the very existence – of the HBC and fought the Royal Adventurers to a standstill.

The NWC was not so much a financial vehicle as a loose confederation of common interests – but it had two major advantages: sheer manpower and the ability to make decisions on the spot rather than awaiting stratagems from overseas. The Nor'Westers, using their birchbark canoes, pushed inland to collect furs directly from Indian trappers and, unlike the more sedentary Bay men, they were constantly in motion. As the beaver lodges in relatively accessible corners were trapped out, the canoes moved ever farther afield. Within twenty years of banding together, the Nor'Westers controlled 78 percent of Canadian fur sales and could caustically claim that the Hudson's Bay Company was doing business "as if drawn by a dead horse."

Later, after the HBC and the NWC had merged under the Charter and name of the HBC, the Company's carefully nurtured domain was overrun by floods of immigrants determined to turn the southern portion of the fur preserve into farmland. The Company adapted, just as it had when challenged by the Nor'Westers, this time building up new monopolies devoted to supplying settlers with their goods and gaining exclusive jurisdiction over water transportation on the Red, Saskatchewan, Athabasca and Mackenzie river systems.

Looking back through the polished brass telescope of imperial history, "the Governor and Company of Adventurers Tradeing into Hudson's Bay," as the Charter characterized the HBC, appears a fiercely patrician enterprise, grandly fielding its own armies and navies, minting its own coins, issuing its own medals, even operating according to a calendar dating from its own creation. Viewed in retrospect, the HBC seems to have been a mercantile mammoth straddling oceans and spanning continents, only recently reduced to more modest circumstances.

Yet for the generations of humble fur traders who scratched for a living in the North American wilderness, the reality was often both harsh and disillusioning. These displaced Scots and Englishmen neither struck metaphorical gold nor found a land to build a dream on.

Nor were there that many of them. Although the French author Jules Verne assured his readers in the novel *The Fur Coun-*

For many years in isolated northern towns, life revolved around the church and the Hudson's Bay post.

try that the Hudson's Bay Company in the early 1870s "employed about a million men in its territories," at the height of its geographical presence, the HBC had fewer than three thousand employees. And as late as 1811 when it was competing head to head with the rambunctious platoons of Nor'Westers fanning out from Montreal, a staff of only 320 was sprinkled throughout its seventy-six posts. The Company covered a lot of territory, but until the mid-twentieth century, its workforce was never very large. The number of Bay men (and women) actually peaked in the early 1980s when its personnel roster nudged 50,000 – an army of clerks and generals as large as the late and glorious East India Company at the height of its powers.

As for financial success, the Company's greatest growth occurred not when it held a monopoly over the fur trade but in much more recent years. Gross revenues first exceeded $1 billion in 1977 and the company's highest profit ($80.3 million) was recorded in 1979. Times turned sour for the Bay in the 1980s, but the Company is still a giant, with more than 400 stores across the country and a wide variety of other real estate holdings.

Hard times have left their mark on the Bay, however. Almost two decades into its fourth century of business, the Company is bleeding, its balance sheet adrift in red ink and its management on edge. Losses amounting to more than $250 million have accumulated since 1981. In 1986, in what was probably the most radical move in its history, the Hudson's Bay Company sold off its fur auction houses in Toronto and London (at the time, the largest in the free world) and the 178 retail outlets it owned in the Canadian North, stores where natives could still barter furs for goods.

In jettisoning these history-laden divisions, the Company shocked some of its most loyal veterans. The Bay had sold its very soul. The gentleman adventurers were being shown the door by cost accountants.

But, more than anything else, even furs, the HBC has always been about survival – survival while huddled on the edge of a vast frozen sea in the middle of a seemingly endless winter, while battling the hard-trading Nor'Westers; survival, even, in a cutthroat world of office towers and pinstripe suits. In selling off the northern stores and auction houses, the Company's managers were prompted by the short-term imperative to reduce the heavy burden of corporate debts. But in the long run they were just exercising the Hudson's Bay Company's will to endure. Judging by its remarkable history, the Company's currently diminished state is only the latest stage in the continuing evolution of the Empire of the Bay.

In winter, the Company's island Waasagomach store in northern Manitoba is accessible by snowmobile.

Empire of the Bay
1610~1870

Pacific Ocean

Gt. Bear Lake

Mackenzie R.

Coppermine R.

Wager Ba

Dubawnt Lake

Gt. Slave Lake

Fort Resolution

Fort Smith

Slave R.

Lake Athabasca

Fort Chipewyan

Fort Prince of Wale

Churchill R.

York Factory

Nelson

Peace R.

Fort McLeod

Fort Edmonton

Cumberland House

Norway House

Bella Coola Inlet

Rocky Moutain House

The Pas

Lake Winnipegosis

Severn R.

Battle R.

N. Saskatchewan R.

Lake Winnipeg

Fraser R.

Okanagan R.

Kootenay R.

S. Saskatchewan R.

Fort Victoria

Fort Garry

Fort St. Charles

Red R.

Fort Vancouver

Columbia R.

Rupert's Land.
Under the terms
of its Charter, the
Company was given
control over all the land
that drained into Hudson Bay.

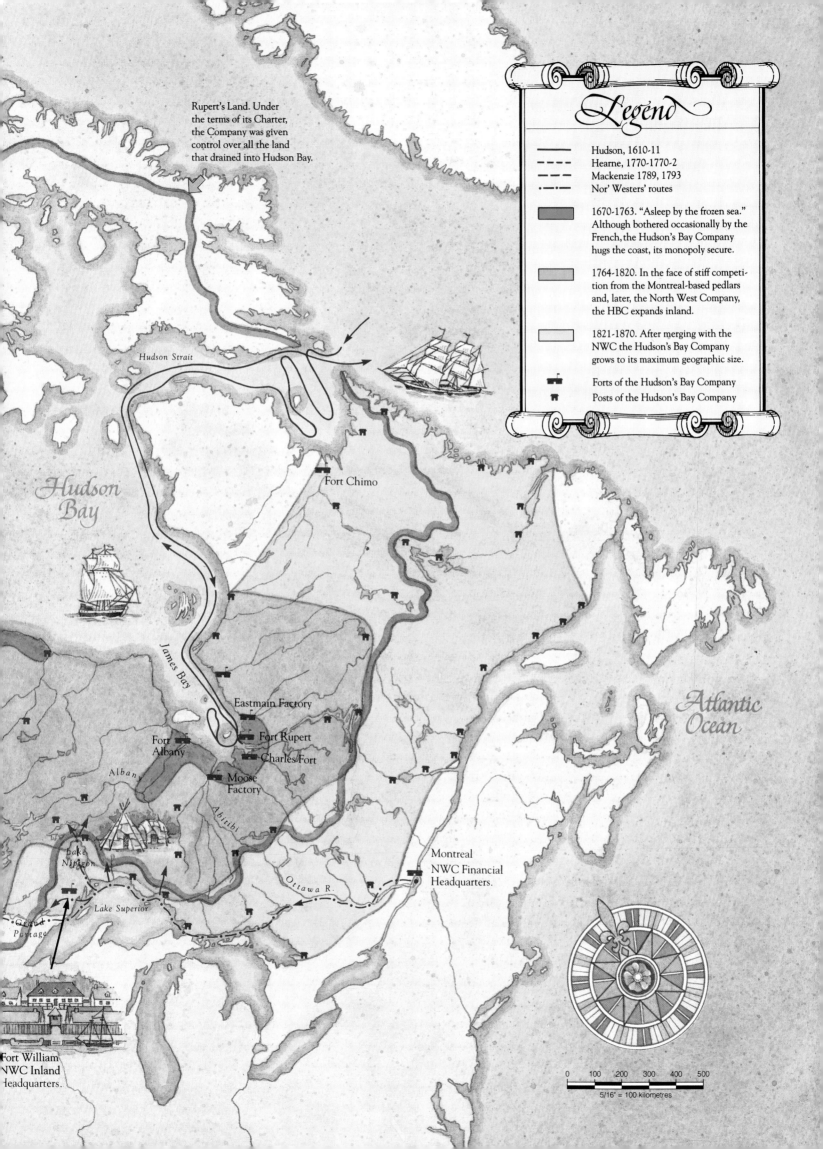

Rupert's Land. Under the terms of its Charter, the Company was given control over all the land that drained into Hudson Bay.

Hudson Strait

Hudson Bay

Fort Chimo

Atlantic Ocean

James Bay

Eastmain Factory

Fort Albany

Fort Rupert

Charles Fort

Moose Factory

Albany

Abitibi

Lake Nipigon

Lake Superior

Grand Portage

Ottawa R.

Montreal NWC Financial Headquarters.

Fort William NWC Inland Headquarters.

0 100 200 300 400 500
5/16" = 100 kilometres

FOR WANT OF A HAT

Beaver hats weren't made of fur but of felt. Beaver fur, specifically the thick, soft undercoat, was sought by hatmakers because of the excellent felt it made. To make a beaver hat, fur was cut away from the pelt and then worked over so that the hairs all lay in the same direction and were of a uniform thickness. Using heat and pressure, this was then pressed, "felted" was the term, into a solid, matted mass. This felt was dyed, stiffened, treated to increase its natural resistance to water, reblocked, ironed and, finally, finished to fit the dictates of current fashion. Properly looked after, a beaver hat could last a lifetime or longer.

(Right) Fashions in beaver hats. The cocked hat gave way in the nineteenth century to the top hat, a design that had its origins in the headgear worn by English Puritans.
(Opposite) A modern London costume supplier shows off a selection of beaver-style hats.

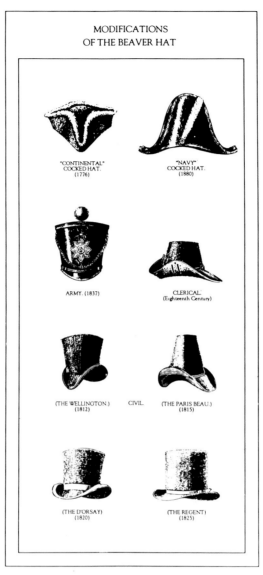

MODIFICATIONS
OF THE BEAVER HAT

"CONTINENTAL" COCKED HAT. (1776)

"NAVY" COCKED HAT. (1880)

ARMY. (1837)

CLERICAL. (Eighteenth Century)

(THE WELLINGTON.) (1812) CIVIL. (THE PARIS BEAU.) (1815)

(THE D'ORSAY) (1820)

(THE REGENT) (1825)

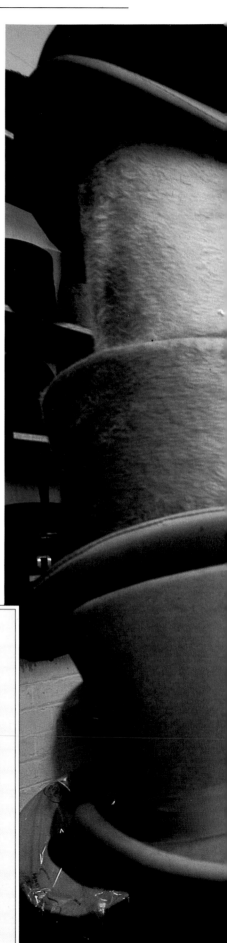

"MAD AS A HATTER"

Lewis Carroll's Mad Hatter was a victim of the beaver hat's popularity. In the early nineteenth century, hat makers, looking for a way to use cheaper furs than the popular beaver, developed a way of turning rabbit fur into a relatively good quality hat-making felt. They used salts of mercury diluted in nitric acid, referred to as a "mercury carrot," to break down the keratin coating on rabbit fur that prevented it from felting properly. The finished rabbit hats were close in quality to beaver, and much cheaper. But there was a drawback:

inhaling the fumes of this mixture led to a condition known as "hatter's shakes," an uncontrollable palsy that also affected the eyes and speech. In the final stages of hatter's shakes, the afflicted hatters went mad, the victims of a mercury-induced psychosis.

(Above) An eighteenth century used-clothes man, wearing his inventory of old beaver hats. Beaver hats were costly investments. As the demand for them grew, a thriving used-hat business evolved.

(Below) A cartoon from the 1700s satirizing extreme hat styles. Adopted by the French court from the highly functional cavalier hats worn by Swedish cavalry in the Thirty Years' War, beaver hats grew over time to impractical proportions.

MARK RICHARD MYERS '88

CHAPTER TWO

VOYAGES INTO THE UNKNOWN

SAILING UNGAINLY THREE-MASTERS WITH THRUSTING bowsprits and taut shrouds, European adventurers cast common sense overboard to embark on improbable voyages into the unknown. It was not a new continent they sought, but cargoes of Oriental silks, precious stones, cinammon and cloves in the golden realms of the Great Khan.

Across their paths lay the Americas, a barrier to their dreams. As they crept northward looking for a way around the cursed continent, seasoned captains quickly learned that the demands of their ambition were not enough to overcome the daunting natural obstacles in their path. Sorely tested by the elements, many survivors never went back to the New World and those who did were humbled anew by their suffering. Only after admitting defeat in their primary quest – reaching Cathay via the great western ocean – did these European freebooters discover other, equally rich cargoes in the New World's creeks and muskeg.

The course westward from Europe was set in the fifteenth century by the scatter-brained Mediterranean mariner Christopher Columbus, who made four journeys to the New World convinced that he had found the "islands at the end of the Orient." Nearly every European monarch whose land was washed by the sea subsequently commissioned navigators to seek landfalls beyond the setting sun. Evidence slowly accumulated to suggest that what they had found was not the far shores of Asia, but a whole new continent. One route round the land barrier was found, through the fogbound and violent Strait of Magellan, but this was two thousand leagues (six thousand miles) longer than a direct route to China – if there were one. For the next three centuries, expeditions varying in skill but equal in gritty determination would try to butt past or through the land barrier blocking easy access to Asia.

The search for this North West Passage began in earnest with the three absurd expeditions of the Elizabethan fortune-hunter Sir Martin Frobisher. A classic English sea-dog in the mould of

(Opposite) A stern view of the Nonsuch, *the first vessel in the North American fur trade.*

Sir Francis Drake, Frobisher took fifteen years to muster enough financial support for his first expedition. Lured by the chance of discovering the mythical North West Passage, he called that cold transit "the only thing of the world which was yet left undone." With the help of Michael Lok, a broker who worked in the City, London's financial district, he at last convinced the directors of the Muscovy Company, a group of merchants engaged in Russian trade, to back his plan. Frobisher's three ships dropped down the Thames tide on June 7, 1576, firing a smoky cannonade as they passed the royal palace at Greenwich. Expectations that Frobisher would return with a hoard of silver from Lima and trunks laden with Manila gold were so firm that Queen Elizabeth I herself subscribed £100 to the expedition.

Off Greenland, one of Frobisher's vessels was swamped by a storm, and its captain, unnerved by the ice, turned back. Twenty-eight days later, while searching the waters west of Greenland aboard the tiny *Gabriel*, Frobisher sighted land and another landfall later appeared to the north. Concluding that the waterway between them was a northern equivalent to the Strait of Magellan, Frobisher's pilot George Best boasted: "So this place he named Frobisher's Straits – like as Magellan at the southwest end of the world, we having discovered the passage to the South Sea." The hapless explorer, convinced he was on his way to the South Seas, was considerably bemused when his progress was halted by an impassable barrier of floating ice.

Once he reached the New World, however, Frobisher's attention was diverted by another discovery. He returned to England carrying a chunk of black rock he had picked up during a brief landfall at Hall Island. Michael Lok's wife happened to toss a chip of it into her dining-room fire, where it burned with a strange flame, and when it was coated in vinegar, it "glisttered with a bright Marquesset of gold." Lok took samples to London assayers who declared it worthless, but an Italian metallurgical charlatan named John Baptiste Agnello pronounced that the rock definitely contained traces of gold. The following April, Frobisher, now bearing the grand title High Admiral, set out again with three ships and twelve dozen miners. His third expedition, in 1578, numbered fifteen ships and four hundred miners. What was agreed to be gold turned out to be common pyrite – fool's gold – and was later put to its only useful purpose as paving stone on London streets. Michael Lok, Frobisher's chagrined patron, landed in debtors' prison but Frobisher himself emerged largely unscathed and served as a vice-admiral with Drake against the Spanish Armada. His greatest

Frobisher's men battle the Eskimos during their 1577 voyage to the New World.

achievement, as it turned out, was having sailed 180 miles into what would later be named Hudson Strait.

Several brief probes into the northern channels followed Frobisher's. While exploring a vast gulf in 1587, a British navigator named John Davis encountered a "furious overfall" – the riptide ebbing out of Hudson Strait. The first Europeans to push beyond the fog-veiled entrance and swirling waters of the strait did so in 1610 under the command of Henry Hudson.

Though infused with the ideals and passion expected of a great explorer, Hudson demonstrated few of the requisite leadership traits. A seasoned mariner with lofty dreams, he became sullen and uncertain when confronted with command decisions. These contradictory characteristics were to fuel his greatest achievements – and seal his tragic fate. A veteran of two attempts to find a *North East* Passage for the Muscovy Company, plus one try at sailing to China via the North Pole, Hudson was hired by the rival Dutch East India Company to ascend the Hudson River in 1609. (That journey led in 1626 to the famous purchase by the Dutch of Manhattan Island from the local Canarsee Indians for trinkets and cloth worth twenty-four dollars.) Hudson's successful exploits brought him to the attention of James I, who would not allow Hudson to return to the Netherlands; it was therefore not the Dutch but a syndicate of English courtiers who sponsored his next voyage, an attempt to chart the North West Passage.

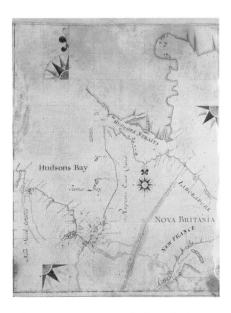

This 1709 map reveals how little was known of the Bay's east coast one hundred years after Henry Hudson had initially explored it.

The expedition, lavishly equipped for its day, was jinxed from the start. The enduring mystery dogging Hudson was why he deliberately gathered such a devil's brew of ill-sorted malcontents to man his ship the *Discovery*, instead of recruiting some of the qualified seamen then readily available for hire on the London docks. Hudson might have been able to meld even this motley assemblage into an effective crew if he had possessed a goodly supply of determination and discipline. Instead, he tried to run his ship democratically by seeking mutual consent for all major decisions.

Sailing into Ungava Bay, the *Discovery* was blocked by ice. Hudson offered to turn back – if the majority wished – but a rogue iceberg interrupted the philosophical musings as captain and crew scrambled to stop the ship from being crushed. His authority undermined, Hudson pressed on, arbitrarily setting a course to the northwest through the treacherous strait that would later bear his name. As soon as Hudson's soundings showed that he was once again in deep open water, his dark spirits lifted. He felt he had won the Passage. Before him lay what seemed open ocean; scuds of water birds mewed their wild calls to beckon him deeper into the deceptive bay.

Tracing the nearly featureless eastern coastline of this unknown sea southward for more than four hundred miles, the *Discovery*'s captain found the shoreline heading gradually west, then suddenly veering south again. This was no course to Cathay; Hudson realized with dawning horror he had reached a dead end. Rather than trying to navigate out of this fairly obvious cul-de-sac, he panicked and began repeatedly criss-crossing what is now James Bay, the southern appendix of Hudson Bay, as the short northern summer drew to a close. Soon it was September and the first winter gales nearly swamped his ship. The first mate, Robert Juet, rebelled. Hudson threw him into irons and appointed a new second-in-command. The crew threatened mutiny. Finally, with the prevailing north winds pushing the *Discovery* towards the low beaches of James Bay, Hudson sought shelter in the shallow waters of a river emptying into what is now Rupert Bay. The ship's carpenter erected a small lean-to of tamarack on the frozen shore as protection for the crew against bitter winter gales.

Because they had believed themselves bound for warmer waters, few of the sailors had brought heavy clothes, and as they huddled in their inadequate shelter, severe frostbite and scurvy became their scourge. The first to die was John Williams, the ship's gunner. The long miserable winter of deaths, disease, petty bickering and vindictive haggling was interrupted only once, by an Indian dragging a sled with two deer carcasses and a pair of beaver hides on it. Hudson traded a knife, a looking-glass and some buttons for the beaver pelts, then huddled down again in the long wait for summer.

It was June before the *Discovery* was free of its icy bonds – but instead of fleeing home across the Atlantic, Hudson resumed his aimless wanderings within the bay. If that weren't enough, he handed out what he claimed was all the remaining hardtack and mouldy cheese but failed to allay suspicions that he had retained a hoard of supplies for himself and his favourites. He then replaced his mate for the second time, substituting Philip Staffe, the ship's illiterate carpenter, thus undermining his authority once again. He also confiscated all the navigation equipment aboard so that his crew could only guess the course he was steering. At that point, the men would take no more. Six days out from their wintering camp, certain that their captain intended to play out what was left of their lives cruising the hated bay, the crew mutinied. The dazed explorer, with his young son John and six loyal crewmen, was bundled into the ship's boat, towed for a short distance, then cut loose.

(Opposite) Hudson and his son adrift as painted by Victorian artist John Collier.

Hudson glares disdainfully at the fleeing mutineers.

The deserted captain raised sail in his lifeboat and, for a time, raced after the mutineers, who were busy looting the ship and gorging on his hidden cache of beer and biscuits. Guilty at the reappearance of their commanding officer, the ship's crew trimmed sail and raced away as if fleeing the devil himself. Hudson and his companions were never seen or heard of again.

Some of the conspirators – including Robert Juet – died during the *Discovery*'s long journey home. Rations exhausted, the starving sailors were reduced to chewing beeswax candlesticks during the voyage's final days. They ceased to care "which end of the ship went forward" yet managed to reach an Irish port. Rather than bring the crewmen to justice immediately, avaricious authorities chose to make use of their newfound knowledge. Two of the original crew members were aboard when the *Discovery* returned to the Arctic in 1612 under the command of Sir Thomas Button. Finally, seven years after Hudson was cast adrift, his crewmen went to trial, charged with murder rather than mutiny. Nothing could be proven and they were acquitted.

Paradoxically, Hudson's journey, tragic and inconclusive as it was, served to inspire others. Over the next two decades, no fewer than ten explorers followed in his wake. All but one, the Dane Jens Munk, were English. The saga of this lone exception is one of the most harrowing in the history of northern exploration.

Munk, who had chased pirates in the North Sea and served in the Danish navy, was ordered by King Christian IV to plot the exact Mercator projections of the North West Passage westward

A woodcut from Jens Munk's account of his 1619 voyage depicting his winter camp at the mouth of what is now the Churchill River.

from Hudson Bay. With a crew of sixty-three aboard two naval ships, Munk set off on May 30, 1619. The voyage to the mouth of the Churchill River was accomplished without incident and the expedition dug in for the winter. Scurvy, caused by a lack of ascorbic acid (Vitamin C), soon began to plague the crews; it loosened teeth and stiffened joints, and then it killed. One by one, Munk's men began to die. In one entry in his log book, Munk wrote his own epitaph: "Herewith, good-night to all the world – and my soul into the hand of God…"

But Munk and two of his men lived to see summer return. The survivors refloated one of the vessels and made their escape in mid-July. In an astounding feat of seamanship, the three Danes sailed safely the 3,500 miles to Copenhagen.

It was with the expeditions of Thomas James and Luke Foxe in 1631 that the dream of the Passage through Hudson Bay at last came to an end. These two voyages mimicked each other, departing within days with identical destinations and similar results. They provided conclusive evidence that the bay's western shore contained no seaway to the Orient. "Even if that merely imaginary passage did exist," James predicted, "it would be narrow, beset by ice, and longer than the route to the east by the Cape." The quest for the Passage, at least for the next century, was over.

Though these early explorers had proved there was no easy water route around this new land via Hudson Bay, there was a growing realization that the Hudson Bay region might hold another prize. James, for one, had noted in his vigorous memoir,

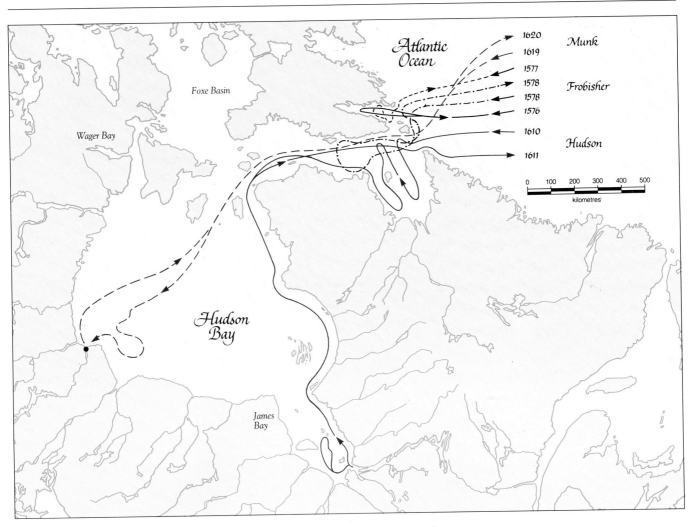

(Top) Early explorers' voyages to Hudson Bay. (Above) Pierre-Esprit Radisson

The Strange and Dangerous Voyage of Captain Thomas James, that those shores were "the home of many of the choicest fur-bearing animals in the world."

Thirty-five years later, in 1666, that intriguing message was delivered to the English court by a pair of wily traders, Pierre-Esprit Radisson and Médard Chouart, Sieur Des Groseilliers.

They stood out among the many fur traders, missionaries, confidence men and royal emissaries sent inland from New France. Among the earliest of Europeans to penetrate deep into the forest belt of the North, Radisson and Groseilliers were the first to negotiate treaties with the Cree, first to explore the upper reaches of the Mississippi and Missouri and first to establish the durable trading pattern into Hudson Bay which was eventually responsible for the creation of the Company of Adventurers.

Their names are almost invariably mentioned in the same breath, but they were very different in age (Radisson was eighteen years the junior), temperament (Groseilliers was the steadfast organizer, Radisson the mercurial merchandiser) and outlook (Radisson wanted to make history, his confrère to forget it). It was Radisson who issued the famous boast of their dominance in the

untamed wilderness: "We were Caesars, being nobody to contradict us."

Radisson and Groseilliers exploring beyond Lake Superior as portrayed by Frederic Remington.

Groseilliers (the name literally meaning "gooseberries" – and that is what generations of Canadian schoolchildren would call him) had arrived in the colony of New France (or Quebec) during his late teens from the Marne country in north-central France. By 1646, the youngster had become a disciple of the Jesuit fathers and served as a lay assistant at their Huron mission near Georgian Bay. Groseilliers returned to Quebec but again visited the land of the Huron from 1654 to 1656 to persuade the Indians to bring more pelts down the St Lawrence. He succeeded, returning with a wealth of furs and stories of rich beaver preserves north of Lake Superior.

Radisson ("radishes" to Groseilliers's "gooseberries") served a more savage apprenticeship. At the age of fifteen while out on a duck shoot, he was ambushed by a band of Mohawks who carried him off to their village on Lake Champlain. Adopted by the family of a warrior who had nineteen white scalps to his credit, Radisson quickly adapted to Mohawk life. He became, in effect, a white Indian, learning their language and skills and joining war parties pillaging the villages of hostile tribes. But sweet memories of New France led him to attempt escape. While hunting with three Mohawks and a captive Algonquin, he and the prisoner escaped after crushing the skulls of their companions. They were quickly tracked and recaptured. The Algonquin was executed on the spot while Radisson was brutally tortured. His soles were seared with heated irons and a red-hot sword was driven through one of his feet. His fingernails were pulled out, then the raw fingertips dipped into canisters of live coals. The village children were just beginning to gnaw on his charred hands when his adoptive family rescued him. The nightmare of that ordeal never left him, and after two more years of captivity he escaped to Fort Orange, a Dutch outpost on the Hudson and, later, to Trois Rivières.

Radisson then joined his new brother-in-law (Groseilliers had married his half-sister) on a fur-trading expedition north of Lake Superior. During the winter of 1659-60, they heard from the Huron, Sioux and Cree of a fortune in beaver furs in the north country and were told of the "Bay of the North," which provided direct access to the region.

The two men returned to New France with rich bales of fur, but the colony's governor, the Marquis d'Argenson, punished them for trading without a licence and rejected their proposal of investigating a possible sea route to the fur country through Hudson Bay.

Angered by the restraints placed on their ambitions by the colonial French bureaucracy, the partners took their dreams elsewhere. In neighbouring New England they aroused interest among local merchants in the idea of mounting expeditions for furs into Hudson Bay. Though these voyages were never completed, they attracted the attention of Colonel George Cartwright, an official of the recently restored Charles II. Cartwright, who had travelled to New England to extract taxes from the new colony, recognized a potential bonanza and, at his urging, the two woodsmen headed for England to seek royal sponsorship.

Radisson and Groseilliers could not have imagined the horrors that awaited their arrival in England. The London they encountered in the autumn of 1665 was in the grip of the dreaded bubonic plague. One-sixth of the city's half-million citizens had already succumbed to the disease. Diarist Samuel Pepys reported the deaths of three to four thousand people a week. On August 12, Pepys wrote: "The people die so, that now it seems they are fain to carry the dead to be buried by daylight, the nights not sufficing to do it in." Save for wandering madmen and assorted prophets of doom, the streets of London were largely deserted as everyone who could—including members of the royal court—fled to the countryside in terror. While travelling by boat up the Thames, Radisson and Groseilliers were given perfumed handkerchiefs to cut the stench of putrefaction coming from the "plague pits" where victims were dumped.

Cold weather finally broke the spread of plague, but another catastrophe followed when, on September 2, 1666, a fire that started in a bakery shop in Pudding Lane engulfed London. Despite the chaos created by these calamities, Charles II found time to meet with the fur traders and was so impressed by the fantastic yarn spun by Radisson and Groseilliers that he granted them royal protection and gave each a weekly pension. The king began to discuss the idea of outfitting a ship for a voyage into Hudson Bay. One of those listening was his cousin Prince Rupert, Duke of Cumberland, Count Palatine of the Rhine and Duke of Bavaria.

In the words of the British historian Hugh Trevor-Roper, Prince Rupert was "a man of intense loyalties but few friends, proud, reserved and morose, uncompromising, unpolitical and undiplomatic, single-minded in his chosen craft of war, which he saw as a personal adventure…. Though he lived long in England, he seemed never to have understood it, or loved it, or its people; only his uncle, Charles I, and – to a lesser extent – his cousin Charles II who, on his restoration, would reward his services with offices and revenues. For the rest, he lived to himself, in a private world, with his blackamoors and his poodles, his books, his laboratory and his instruments of art."

Prince Rupert

An incongruous blend of Sir Galahad and Cyrano de Bergerac, Rupert provided the needed spark to bring the Company of Adventurers to life and keep it going during its first frail dozen years, sustaining the royal patronage and romantic impulse without which the tiny enterprise would have foundered. Born in 1619, Rupert was the son of Frederick V, Elector Palatine and (as Frederick I) King of Bohemia, and Elizabeth Stuart, daughter of King James I of England. In 1620, with the outbreak of the Thirty Years' War, his family was forced to throw itself on the fiscal mercies of its English royal relatives. Young Rupert was granted a royal pension of £300 by England's Charles I – a gift the prince would pay back in service many times over.

Not as prominent or as well understood as he deserves to be, Rupert is remembered largely as the most successful Royalist cavalry officer of the English Civil War. But there was much more to the dark and handsome Prince than mere cavalier flash. Exiled from England after the defeat of the Royalists by Cromwell, Rupert took hold of the remnants of the royalist fleet and began to prey on English shipping. After the Restoration, and his return to England, he was given naval command during three minor wars with the Dutch.

One of the few military men equally at home in the world of ideas, his many inventions included fashioning a primitive torpedo, the forerunners of the modern revolver and machine gun, tear-shaped glass globules known as Rupert's drops which led to the making of bulletproof glass, a naval quadrant that made it possible to take observations at sea in rough weather, and a "diving engine" used successfully to retrieve sunken treasure. In his alternative incarnation as an artist, Rupert worked out a new means of drawing buildings in perspective and a technique for painting on marble, but his main artistic achievement was to introduce in England the art of mezzotint, a novel method of engraving.

It was in the capacity of entrepreneur that Prince Rupert met with Radisson and Groseilliers at Windsor Castle, listening with mounting excitement as Radisson described the fur harvest and copper outcrops he had glimpsed in the lands north of Superior. The Prince was captivated by the prospect of an empire's worth of riches beyond Hudson Bay and became determined to wrest the lucrative North American fur trade from the French. He began organizing a private syndicate to finance an exploratory journey to Hudson Bay.

Once investment monies were in place, the Prince persuaded Charles to lease to the enterprise a two-masted ketch, the *Eaglet*, for a nominal sum. A second, smaller vessel, the forty-five-ton former Royal Navy ketch *Nonsuch*, was purchased for £290. By May 1668 the expedition had been outfitted; grocers, chandlers, sailmakers, ropemakers, vintners, butchers, haberdashers, timber merchants and ironmongers furnished the two ships for the journey. Radisson sailed with Captain William Stannard aboard the *Eaglet* and Groseilliers sailed with Captain Zachariah Gillam on the *Nonsuch* . Their instructions called for the *Eaglet* to winter in the bay while the *Nonsuch* carried home the pelts from the first summer's trade, before returning again with provisions.

After a farewell banquet in his Spring Gardens home, Rupert and the syndicate members were rowed down the Thames to see the ships off at Gravesend. On the misty morning ebb-tide of June 3, 1668, the tiny vessels were piloted down the river. By evening they had reached open sea and set sail northward in a fresh breeze for the New World.

Four hundred leagues off Ireland, a storm almost swamped the low-waisted *Eaglet*, forcing her to turn back. The *Nonsuch* persevered and anchored in Hudson Bay that August.

Despite heavy seas that turned back her sister ship the Eaglet, *the* Nonsuch *arrived safely in Hudson Bay.*

A camp was established at the mouth of the very same river on James Bay where Hudson had spent his wretched winter, but this time the crews were ready for the season's fury. A stockade and house were fashioned out of spruce trees and a cellar dug below the frost line to store beer. Provisions carried by the expedition were augmented by local fish and game. Thus prepared, the crewmen settled into their tiny fort to await the spring. They developed a touch of scurvy but no lives were lost. The severe effects of the disease were warded off by lemon juice from aboard ship and Groseilliers's bitter-tasting concoctions of spruce beer.

In April, nearly three hundred James Bay Indians came to trade. A "League of Friendship" was struck with the local chief and the land was "formally purchased" while British muskets, hatchets, scrapers, needles and trinkets were profitably traded for the valuable beaver pelts. By October 1669, the fur-laden *Nonsuch* was home, her arrival signalling that the illusion of a northern route to the riches of the Orient had given way to another daring scheme – the establishment of a monopoly over a kingdom of fur.

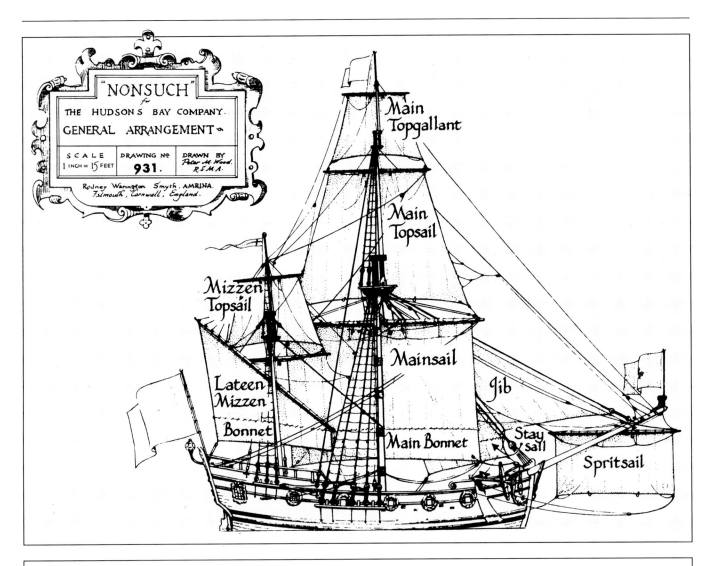

NONSUCH

for

THE HUDSON'S BAY COMPANY.

GENERAL ARRANGEMENT.

SCALE
1 INCH = 15 FEET

DRAWING No
931.

DRAWN BY
Peter M. Wood.
R.S.M.A.

Rodney Warrington Smyth. AMRINA.
Falmouth, Cornwall, England.

Main Topgallant

Main Topsail

Mizzen Topsail

Mainsail

Jib

Lateen Mizzen

Main Bonnet

Stay 'sail

Bonnet

Spritsail

THE NONSUCH

A cramped fifty-three feet long, the *Nonsuch* was outfitted as a virtual floating department store for her trip into Hudson Bay. Hundreds of trade items, including thirty-seven pounds of tobacco and four dozen pairs of shoes, shared space with eleven men. The *Nonsuch*'s career in the fur trade was brief. After her return to England in 1669, she was sold for £152.

(Right) A cutaway view. Most of the crew would have squeezed in forward of the two large cargo holds.
(Opposite) The Nonsuch replica under sail. This accurate reconstruction was built in 1970 on the HBC's 300th anniversary.

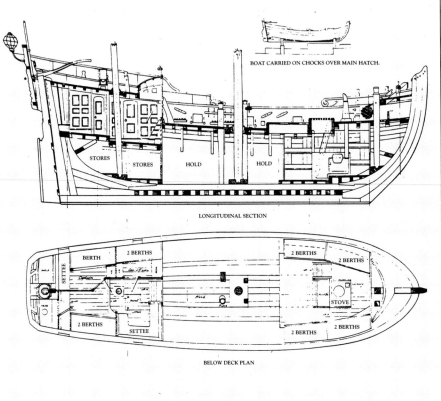

BOAT CARRIED ON CHOCKS OVER MAIN HATCH.

STORES   STORES   HOLD   HOLD

LONGITUDINAL SECTION

BERTH   2 BERTHS   2 BERTHS   2 BERTHS

SETTEE   STOVE

2 BERTHS   SETTEE   2 BERTHS   2 BERTHS

BELOW DECK PLAN

CHAPTER THREE

LORDES AND PROPRIETORS

CHARLES II'S ROYAL CHARTER FORMING THE "GOVERnor and Company of Adventurers of England tradeing into Hudson's Bay" was the most generous land grant ever presented by a monarch to a subject. Hudson Bay and the vast lands of its drainage basin were awarded to Charles's "dear and entirely beloved cousin" Prince Rupert and his fellow Adventurers as "true and absolute Lordes and Proprietors" of an unexplored overseas empire.

By setting the geographical limits of the territory at the head of all streams draining into Hudson Bay, the grant enclosed a subcontinent of 1.5 million square miles, its eastern boundary extending back to the height of land in the far reaches of Labrador and down to the Precambrian ridges above the headwaters of the St Lawrence's tributaries. It swept south past the 49th parallel and west through the Red River Valley to the peaks of the Rocky Mountain divide.

Named Rupert's Land, this huge freehold was the equivalent of nearly 40 percent of modern Canada, plus much of the American states of Minnesota and North Dakota. Even these boundaries did not define the limits set out in the document. The Charter in effect granted a monopoly over trade originating anywhere west of Hudson Bay, so that if the North West Passage had actually existed where navigators of that day placed it, the HBC would have possessed control of trading rights, based on discovery, all the way to the shores of Cathay.

When the five sheepskin parchment sheets bearing seven thousand words of text received royal assent on Friday, May 2, 1670, in Whitehall Palace, the Company had briefly touched only the periphery of its holdings. The fragile enterprise faced a daunting task in its first decades: to stake out forts at the mouths of the great rivers that empty into Hudson Bay and maintain them despite the region's wretched climate and the protracted efforts by the French to capture the outposts by force of arms.

(Opposite) Investors greet the Nonsuch *on her return to London, October 1669.*

The return of the fur-loaded *Nonsuch* to London in 1669 had caused minimal stir; its cargo, bartered for goods originally purchased for £650, brought £1,379 on the London fur market while the ship was resold for £152. Wages of £535 plus the required start-up investments, custom duties, the damage to the *Eaglet* and other expenses made the voyage unprofitable, but its backers were delighted. Radisson and Groseilliers had been vindicated: it was entirely practical to sail into Hudson Bay, winter on its shores and return with a potentially profitable cargo of fur.

Rupert interceded repeatedly with Charles II on the Company's behalf, procuring, for example, the loan of a larger ship, the *Wivenhoe*. The minutes of early board meetings record gifts of "beaver stockings for the King," "silver tankards, hogsheads of claret" and "cat skin counterpanes for his bed" to the Company's powerful friends. At fifty-one, Rupert was becoming such an idol to English commerce that a few months after the return of the *Nonsuch* the soldier-scientist was invited to lay the cornerstone of London's new Royal Exchange.

Charles II signing the Charter of the Company of Adventurers.

Four weeks after the HBC was awarded its Charter, the *Wivenhoe* and the *Prince Rupert*, a seventy-five-ton frigate commissioned especially for the fur trade, cast away from Ratcliffe Wharf below the Tower, under orders to establish a permanent trading post on Hudson Bay's Nelson River.

Prince Rupert and the newly incorporated Committeemen tendered a boisterous farewell banquet to the voyage's leaders: Zachariah Gillam, formerly of the *Nonsuch* and now skipper of the *Prince Rupert*, which also carried Groseilliers; Robert Newland, commander of the *Wivenhoe*, with Radisson aboard; and their newly chosen overseas Governor, Charles Bayley, who had only recently been released from the Tower of London to lead the royal treasure hunt.

The choice of Bayley – the only Governor of an overseas English protectorate ever installed in his position straight out of jail – was peculiar. A Quaker convert who had vague connections with the Stuarts, Bayley had been jailed for eccentric acts, including a bizarre attempt to convert the Pope to Protestantism and, upon returning to England, for refusing to take the oath of allegiance. From various dungeons he wrote lengthy epistles to Charles II, warning the king of dangers to his throne and cautioning that unless the monarch avoided "rioting and excess, chambering and wantonness" he would be "threatened with a share in the whirlwind of the Lord" that was coming to the nation. An unenthusiastic royal response left Bayley languishing in the Tower of London for seven years, where fellow prisoners described him as "an old Quaker with a long beard," teetering on the edge of madness.

The discredited zealot was released from the Tower on condition that he "betook himself to the navigation of Hudson Bay and the places lately discovered and to be discovered in those parts." A very changed Bayley sailed out in command of the first expedition under Company colours, landed at the estuary of the Nelson River and nailed the King's Arms to a tree to claim the territory. Bayley had time for little more than expeditious formalities before an autumn gale forced the *Wivenhoe* back into deep water. Her captain decided to winter 720 miles away across the bay at Charles Fort (soon renamed Rupert House), where the *Prince Rupert* was already safely braced for winter.

The bay-side Governor confirmed the treaties Gillam and Groseilliers had negotiated with local Indians the previous season and the little colony settled in for the mandatory hibernation. Scurvy was kept to a minimum that winter with generous daily quaffs of spruce brew, though the captain of the *Wivenhoe* and his mate died of influenza. The Indians who braved the snows to barter for much-coveted steel knives and iron axes brought not only furs but fresh deer meat, wild fowl, sturgeon, whitefish and trout. Life took on reasonably civilized overtones as the sailors baked venison pie and pickled the fall geese in brine. After spring breakup, two small boats were launched to range down the coast, where Bayley and Radisson were able to trade for beaver skins at the mouth of the Moose River.

The first fur auction. For several seasons after 1672, the bidding was conducted at Garraway's Coffee House in the City of London.

Over the next nine years, with only one brief interruption, Bayley conducted the business of the fledgling Company with imagination and sound judgment, establishing its influence at the estuaries of the major rivers flowing into James and Hudson bays. It was Bayley who staked out the matrix of the Company's "factory" system, which meant that trade could be carried on from coastal forts instead of from aboard ship, an arrangement that allowed the Company to maintain constant contact with its customers.

The confident progress of the young Company left Radisson and Groseilliers feeling isolated and unappreciated. Their every suggestion that its trade be carried into the interior met with suspicious whispers that they were really determined to desert the English and entrust their knowledge to the French. Influenced by the stern invocations of the visiting Jesuit Charles Albanel, offers of four hundred Louis-d'or and restoration of their former estates, plus the promise that their woods lore would be more profitably employed in the service of France, they did indeed switch sides in 1674.

Wee Doe Grant
unto the said Governor and
Company and theire successors the
sole Trade and Commerce of all
those Seas Streightes Bayes Rivers
Lakes Creekes and Soundes that
lie within the entrance of
Hudsons Streightes and
make create and constitute (them)
the true and absolute Lordes and
Proprietors of the same
Territory

Within the next eight years, the HBC would suffer two other serious losses. Bayley's term came to an abrupt end when he was recalled to London and accused of unspecified irregularities. He died before he could clear his name, and two years later Prince Rupert collapsed while attending a theatre performance. His condition was diagnosed as pleurisy with a high fever, and when the HBC Committee next met to re-elect Rupert as Governor he did not have the strength to attend. On November 29, 1682, Rupert died – just short of his sixty-third birthday – still adamantly refusing to be bled and expiring fully in command of himself. No monument survives to mark Rupert's tomb. Only a bittersweet epitaph identifies the final resting place of the Hudson's Bay Company's founder and first Governor. "A soldier's life is a life of honour," it reads, "but a dog would not lead it."

A dozen years after the granting of its Charter, the Company was generating a yearly profit of 200 percent on invested capital and was only two years away from declaring its first hefty dividend. The problem was finding a worthy successor to Prince Rupert.

The Committeemen approached James, Duke of York, brother to the king and his successor. With his acceptance, the Company found itself temporarily on the winning side of the struggle for the English Crown, although the Duke of York proved to be as ineffective a Governor as he was later king of England. His lack of enthusiasm for the HBC stemmed in part from his desire to stay on good terms with Louis XIV of France and the conflict of interest he felt from his ownership of competing beaver preserves in the upper reaches of the Hudson River Valley.

The only good thing about the Duke of York's tenure was its brevity – just two years, from January 1683 to February 1685, at which point he resigned to become king of England. The sole other mention of James II in Company minutes occurs on October 31, 1688, when Sir Edward Dering, then Deputy Governor, paid the king his HBC dividend of 150 guineas in gold. Five days later, fleeing from William of Orange and the "Glorious Revolution," James left England.

The Duke of York's flaccid stewardship and the strain in relations between France and England prompted the Committeemen to seek as his successor a solidly well-connected candidate for the HBC governorship. There was one obvious choice: the Right Honourable John, Lord Churchill (later Duke of Marlborough). Second son of an impoverished Stuart administrator, he rose from being a lowly page to the Duke of York to become the power behind the British throne, attaining a phenomenal array of titles and honours along the way; his stunning success in ten major military

John, Lord Churchill (later the Duke of Marlborough) became the HBC's third Governor in 1685.

(Previous Page) The Hudson's Bay Company Charter shown against a panoramic view of the Hayes River.

campaigns set the tone for two centuries of successful British imperialism. According to Sir Winston Churchill, his splendid descendant nine generations removed, the Duke had been "a greater do-er than he was a man," but there is little doubt that during his seven years as the HBC's Governor, Marlborough rescued the Company from the neglect of his predecessor and placed it on a comfortable political footing. If Rupert was the HBC's princely founder, the Duke of Marlborough was its noble preserver, for it was he who assured the fledgling enterprise of his protection while he was broadening and consolidating his civilian and military power base. One significant achievement of his stewardship was parliamentary confirmation of the Company's Charter, which had never received Parliament's approbation. Despite spirited lobbying for the abolition of the HBC's monopoly by competing interests, Parliament passed an act confirming its Charter in 1690.

A more serious threat to the Company's monopoly on the bay grew out of the war between England and France. The HBC trading posts became regal pawns in the escalating hostilities, and even though the writ of European monarchs carried little sanction on the gravelly shores of the bay, the traders who manned the wilderness forts found themselves caught up in a fight not of their own making. French flotillas and overland raiding parties from Montreal attacked and pillaged the HBC's fur factories. Because the HBC traders were far more interested in staying alive to collect their pay than in sacrificing their lives to defend corporate storehouses of pungent pelts, they accepted defeat with more relief than shame. Some of the posts changed hands half a dozen times.

While the battles for Hudson Bay were being waged, the price of beaver pelts on European markets dropped, mainly because of overproduction from New York and other colonies. Because of this glut, the HBC fought back just hard enough to maintain a toehold on the bay – keeping only one post in its possession at a time (either Albany or York) – and concentrated instead on lobbying royal courtiers at the courts of St James's and Versailles. Even so, the hollow boom of cannon fire and the terror of guerrilla attacks on the inadequately armed forts became commonplace on the once ignored bay. Radisson had meanwhile allied himself with an unusually talented financier from Amiens named Charles Aubert de La Chesnaye, and the pair formed La Compagnie du Nord as New France's thorny challenge to the HBC. In return for a quarter of the profits, Radisson had agreed to lead an expedition to Hudson Bay. By 1682, La Chesnaye had organized a flotilla of two small ships and twenty-seven men to carry Radisson and Groseilliers with orders to establish Compagnie du Nord's first permanent

An early nineteenth-century view of Albany Factory, located on the west coast of James Bay.

45

station at the mouth of the Hayes River. Radisson had camped at the nearby Nelson River with Charles Bayley a decade earlier and was aware that the upper reaches of the Hayes were connected to the wider Nelson; he also knew that because the smaller stream was easier to navigate, most natives preferred to switch to it on the final leg of their journey down to the bay. The adjacent estuaries of these two rivers, whose sources were hundreds of miles upstream in prime fur country, were the site of the bay's major battles, and York Factory, the post that sprouted there, quickly became the area's main settlement.

Outmanned and outgunned, Radisson drew on raw luck, plus the threat of non-existent French troops supposedly lurking just beyond the horizon, to disarm first a group of independent traders from Boston and then a shipload of HBC men, including John Bridgar, appointed York's first Governor. Appropriating two thousand pelts that had been traded during the winter, Radisson and Groseilliers sailed off in triumph for Quebec – but once again their hopes were betrayed by the authorities of New France. Officials confiscated their ships and charged them the standard 25 percent duty exacted on local fur catches. That was enough frustration for the worn-out Groseilliers, who in 1683, aged sixty-five, retired to his modest seigneury at Trois Rivières, where he died peacefully in 1696.

Instead of pulling back, Radisson began to plot his revenge through reconciliation with his former English employers. One British emissary who negotiated with Radisson in France described him as being "apparelled more like a savage than a Christian." But the HBC was anxious to have the woodsman back and Radisson was easily seduced by their overtures, confiding in his journal: "I yielded to these solicitations and am determined to go to England forever, and so strongly bind myself to his Majesty's service…that no other cause could ever detach me from it." He was welcomed back to London by the HBC Committeemen, who swallowed their scepticism after he revealed that his nephew was still in Port Nelson guarding a magnificent hoard of skins awaiting shipment. Rewarded with a silver tankard, £200 in Company stock and the grand if slightly hollow title of Superintendent and Chief Director of Trade at Port Nelson, he sailed again for the bay, this time aboard the aptly named *Happy Return*. His arrival under English colours understandably confused his patient nephew, who had by then garnered a valuable booty of twenty thousand pelts – a treasure he was now being asked to turn over to the hated Hudson's Bay Company.

Radisson repeated his lucrative visits to the bay for three more years, but by the close of the seventeenth century, he was sixty-four years old and being only vaguely credited for his exploits on the Company's behalf. Penny-pinching Committeemen with short memories cut his pension, and it took him five years of tedious legal procedures to win it back. The one-time Caesar of the wilderness was reduced to begging the Company for a job as its London warehouse-keeper; he was turned down. Pierre-Esprit Radisson died in 1710, aged seventy-four, his zest for life extinguished, his grave unmarked.

His defection hadn't dampened French interest in the bay, where the HBC posts were returning £20,000 annually and diverting a growing proportion of the trade that had originally gone to Montreal. La Compagnie du Nord had little trouble persuading Brisay de Denonville, governor of New France, to mount a military expedition overland to capture the forts of the English intruders. An army of seventy Canadian irregulars, a few native guides, thirty French soldiers and their leader, the Chevalier de Troyes, set out from Montreal in March 1686 on an eight-hundred-mile journey that remains an epic of bush travel. First they stole up on the HBC's Moose Factory and captured it with little resistance. The solo stand of one of de Troyes's deputies, the twenty-four-year-old Pierre Le Moyne d'Iberville, was the most dramatic moment in the brief scrap. Finding himself inside the fort with the gate shut behind him, he held off the entire garrison – sword in one hand and musket in the other – until his companions forced the gateway open again and captured the post.

The next fort to fall to the French was Rupert House, seventy-five miles up the east coast of James Bay, and along with it went the supply ship *Craven*, which was anchored nearby. The *Craven* was in turn used against the British in the assault on the more heavily armed HBC fortress at the mouth of the Albany River. De Troyes and d'Iberville took ashore the heavy siege guns they had brought from Rupert House, mounted them on a patch of frozen gravel outside the palisade and patiently lobbed 140 shots into the fort. As the attacking troops shouted *Vive le Roi!*, an echo of their war cry could be faintly heard – so faintly, in fact, that d'Iberville realized it was emanating from the fort's cellar where the timorous defenders were huddled in refuge instead of firing back. The cannonade stopped only when the bravest Englishman present made an unexpected appearance. Through the gate the resident chaplain hove into sight, holding high a maid's white apron tied to his walking stick.

(Above) Pierre Le Moyne d'Iberville. (Top, right) The seige of York Factory in 1697 by d'Iberville's gunners.

With sufficient men left behind to guard the spoils, the victorious de Troyes and d'Iberville returned to Quebec. But d'Iberville was soon on the move again – to France this time, where he obtained a fast new frigate, the *Soleil d'Afrique*. Not yet thirty, he had been appointed Commander-in-Chief of Hudson Bay. After several minor naval skirmishes in the bay over the next few years, the king of France in 1697 dispatched the most formidable fleet ever sent to Hudson Bay. In the greatest Arctic sea battle in North American history, Royal Navy men-of-war assigned by Britain to support the HBC claims clashed with the French over who was to hold the lucrative post of York Factory. The engagement, decisively won by the French, should have consolidated d'Iberville's international reputation; since the battle-prize was merely a fur trading post on the margin of civilization, however, his remarkable exploits were largely ignored.

Under the command of d'Iberville aboard the forty-four-gun *Pélican*, the French ships were stuck for three weeks among the floes blocking Hudson Strait. When the flagship finally bucked free, she laid a southwesterly course and by September 3 reached the Nelson River and dropped anchor. The following morning at 9:30, just after he had sent a shallop ashore with twenty-five men to reconnoitre the British-held fortress, d'Iberville spied the silhouettes of three peaked sails on the horizon. Certain that this was the balance of his fleet, he raised anchor and sailed out to meet his mates, yardarms aflutter with signal flags. No response. The trio of newcomers was almost alongside his gunwales when he realized that this was an enemy fleet: two armed freighters – the *Dering* and the *Hudson's Bay* – flying the flag of the Company of Adventurers, and a proud man-o'-war, the Royal Navy frigate *Hampshire*. Among them, the English ships boasted 118 guns and full complements of sailors and marines, while the *Pélican* was emphatically short-handed with some of her best soldiers ashore and

others weak with scurvy. As d'Iberville swept by the *Hampshire*, Captain John Fletcher, its commanding officer, let go a broadside that left the *Pélican*'s rigging in tatters, and the two HBC ships poured a stream of grapeshot and musket fire into the unprotected stern.

The battle raged for four hours. It looked for a time as if d'Iberville had lost. The blood of the wounded French sailors bubbled down the clinkerboards through the scuppers into the sea. In a brief respite, Fletcher called across to demand d'Iberville's surrender. When the Frenchman refused, the English captain paid tribute by toasting his courage with vintage wine. Minutes later, d'Iberville let go a broadside of his own, and the *Hampshire* went down with all hands. The *Hudson's Bay* let go one more volley and surrendered, and the *Dering* made a dash for shelter.

With the fall of York Factory, France had at least temporarily won the battle for the bay. For the next sixteen years, the HBC Committeemen stewed and plotted how to win back their royal monopoly of the region's riches.

D'Iberville's ship the Pélican *battling the* Hampshire.

49

YORK FACTORY

It was called a "factory" because the "factor," the Company's regional man-in-charge, lived there. Located halfway up the west coast of Hudson Bay, York Factory was established as one of the HBC's first permanent trading stations in 1684 and named after the Company's Governor, the Duke of York. Over the next two centuries, interrupted only by attacks from the French, virtually all the trade goods and furs moving in and out of the Company's vast holdings passed through York Factory.

By the mid 1800s the Factory had become a township of thirty buildings laid out in an H-shape, with the main depot and guest houses forming the centre. Its wings included the doctor's house, a hospital, library, cooperage, bakehouse, various fur stores, provisions houses and officers' and servants' quarters. Above it all, on a flagstaff of Norway pine, snapped the Company flag.

(Opposite and above) Only the deserted white depot building remains today in marked contrast to the busy complex that existed in 1880 (left) fronted with vegetable gardens that had been cultivated for over a century despite the thin soil and short growing season.

(Bottom) York Factory in 1853 from a sketch by Chief Trader A.H. Murray.

CHAPTER FOUR

ASLEEP BY THE FROZEN SEA

"THERE IS NOTHING MORE PERSISTENT IN THE WORLD than these claims of the Hudson's Bay Company. We are desirous greatly to see all these smug ancient gentlemen satisfied," complained Lord Bolingbroke, leader of the British treaty negotiations with France at Utrecht following the thirteen-year War of the Spanish Succession.

The HBC Committeemen certainly proved more adept at the game of diplomacy than they had at fighting distant wars, for the Company won back at the bargaining table the posts it had lost during the battle for the bay. When the Treaty of Utrecht was signed in 1713, the Sun King's representatives resigned themselves not only to "cession" of Newfoundland but to the full restoration of the Hudson's Bay Company's territories. The treaty inaugurated an unprecedented thirty-one years of peace between France and England and boldly signposted the HBC's "title" to exclusive use of its huge overseas territories.

That ownership of the wilderness around Hudson Bay could become the subject of two articles in the Treaty of Utrecht was more a triumph of obstinacy by the Company's petitioners than a measure of its importance as real estate in the conduct of Britain's *realpolitik*. The day-to-day bustle of the City fur markets and London docksides in 1713 seemed only tenuously connected to the sealed royal parchments of 1670 and the glory of the Restoration courtier statesmen who had originally formed the Company of Adventurers.

War had been bad for business. Unable to pay its tradesmen, the Company found it had to dip into the vaults of its bankers to settle wartime excise bills and was reduced to the desperate expedient of borrowing to pay interest on existing debt. Anthony Beale, the Governor of its only surviving fort, Albany, was owed £600 in back pay. According to historian E.E. Rich, the HBC's survival at the turn of the eighteenth century depended on "the connivance of a bankrupt Governor," Sir Stephen Evans, whose

(Opposite) A native trapper and his dog pass by Fort Prince of Wales in the early 1700s.

erratic tenure ended in 1712 when he cheated his creditors one last time by committing suicide.

Two years later, the HBC sent veteran administrator James Knight to reclaim York Factory from its French occupiers. Bearing a royal mandate which owed its authority to the terms of Utrecht, he found a quaint cluster of rickety shacks manned by a wretched crew of just nine French defenders, including a chaplain, a surgeon and an apprentice. In a vivid dispatch to his principals in London, Knight complained that York's facilities were "nothing but a confused heap of old rotten houses without form or strength very not sufficient to secure your goods from the weather, not fit for men to live in without being exposed to the frigid weather."

With Albany Fort, the reoccupied and rebuilt York Factory and a scattering of trading depots, the HBC reimposed its presence on the bay. Instead of vigorously expanding its trade by moving inland, the Company was content to drift into what one disillusioned officer later labelled its long "Sleep by the Frozen Sea." Without the threat of competition, the inclination of the Company's officers was to squat quietly on the periphery of the bay and let the Indians bring the furs to them.

The dynamics of the fur trade grew static, if not altogether comatose. Hardly anything interrupted its monotonous rhythm. The financial reporting and management methods put in place by Sir Bibye Lake functioned as if the HBC Governor, who served from 1712 to 1743, had invented a money machine. As long as the Company's profits were reflected in respectable dividends and the Indians continued to fetch furs, there was no particular need to expand the Company's activities, no purpose in searching for the North West Passage or exploring the hinterland.

The extended domination of the Lake family – particularly the tenure of Sir Bibye – was marked by consolidation, efficiency and prosperity, but also by a narrowness of outlook quite contrary to the buccaneering instincts of the original Adventurers. The real paradox of Lake's remarkable career was how, without venturing farther from London than his country estate, he was able to instill in the HBC factors, an ocean away, his stubbornly maintained corporate ethic. In this he was aided by the constancy of the seasonal and commercial cycles into which life on Hudson Bay was divided, and the unchanging nature of the quest for fur.

Hudson Bay may be an inland sea nearly as large as the Mediterranean – its shoreline meanders for 7,600 miles, a distance only 300 miles shorter than the earth's diameter at the equator – but during most of the eighteenth century, the HBC Governors kept fewer than two hundred men posted there to exploit their

The interior of a Cree wigwam belonging to what were called "home guard" Indians because they chose to settle near Hudson's Bay posts. They also acted as middlemen for the Company, trading with inland tribes.

immense holdings. John Oldmixon, in his 1708 study *The British Empire in America*, admitted that he should have led off his book with a description of the Hudson's Bay Company's territories, but explained, "There being no Towns nor Plantations in this Country, but two or three poor Forts to defend the Factories, we thought we were at Liberty to place it where we pleas'd, and were loath to let our History open with the Description of so miserable a Wilderness."

Life in these northern outposts of the Empire was never easy. Because it is out of reach of moderating ocean currents, Hudson Bay is more frigid than the iceberg-packed Arctic Ocean or the North Pole itself. Temperatures of -82°F have been recorded, colder than most polar lows. For nine months of the year, the sun hugs the horizon, the fierce winds snarl across the beaches and eskers; on overcast days drifting snow creates a disorienting white void that obliterates all points of reference. "Rich as the trade to these parts have been or may be," wrote John Oldmixon, "the way of living is such that we can not reckon any man happy whose lot is cast upon this Bay...for that country is so prodigiously cold that nature is never impregnated by the sun; or, rather, her barren womb produces nothing for the subsistence of man."

Factors' journal entries bore vivid witness to the awesome furies of a bay winter: "Insufferable cold. Almost froze my arm in bed"; "Very troublesome to write, ink freezing on my pen"; "Frozen feet and no wonder, as the thermometer for the last three nights was -36, -42 and -38"; "Men cannot see a hundred yards to windward – neither can one get out of our gates for snow"; "Some quicksilver that had been put out some time ago for trying the cold was observed to be frozen while the thermometer was only 36 below zero, which proves the weather to have been six degrees colder than per thermometer"; "Rain froze as it fell – if we have one hour fine weather, we have ten bad for it"; "Hail the size of a Musket Ball"; "Twenty-one years in this country and never see or hear so dismal a night.... "

The brief summers brought little respite. Temperatures could rise as high as 80°F, but the numbing agony of the winter's cold was replaced by intolerable plagues of "mosketos" and "sand flyes." While he was at Churchill, James Knight gave way to near-hysteria in his August 11, 1717, journal entry describing the hellish insects: "Here is now such swarms of a small sand flyes that wee can hardly see the sun through them.... They fly into our ears nose eyes mouth and down our throats as we be most sorely plagued with them.... Certainly these be the flyes that was sent as plagues to

Ships entering the Hayes River near York Factory in preparation for winter. Any vessel staying the winter had to be anchored upriver to avoid the Bay's treacherous ice.

the Egyptians as caused a darkness over the land and brought such blotches and boils as broke out over them into sores."

Knight, who dominated the HBC's overseas history during the first two decades of the eighteenth century, also penned the classic definition of another of the region's peculiarities, permafrost, when he noted that "the summer never thaws above the depth of what the following winter freezes."

The grim demands of survival forced life on the bay into a dreary routine. Endurance was the prime virtue. Like the animal inhabitants of some isolated Darwinian island, the Bay traders assumed local coloration, appearing, according to York Factor James Isham, "more like beasts than men, with the hairy cloathing we wear."

Winter dress consisted of a combination of pelts that made the Hudsonians resemble a surrealistic mutation of every fur-bearing animal within trapping range. The outer garment was of moose-skin, with cuffs and a cape of beaver, marten or fox. Breeches were cut from deerskin and lined with flannel over three layers of cut-up blankets. Shoes consisted of a shaped piece of tough leather wrapped around the instep and fastened securely. That ensemble, which made limb movements ponderous, was in fact the standard *indoor* uniform; it was merely underwear for the outdoors. Winter wood- and food-gathering excursions required the addition of yet more clothing, and even then limbs and faces often froze.

Hunger was one of the few human appetites that could safely and prodigiously be satisfied within the cramped world of the Bay. Anxious to fill the pages of their journals, Factors often described menus at their posts, detailing the remarkable quantity, if not variety, of the food consumed. James Knight at York Factory recorded that during three days of feasting at Christmas in 1715, he allocated to each mess hall of four men a helping of four geese, a large slice of beef, four hares, seven pounds of fresh pork, two pounds of drippings, a pound of butter, three and a half pounds of fruit preserves, four pounds of flour and a hogshead of strong beer. This was special fare, but the daily rations were only slightly more modest. Provisioning was partly from the holds of the annual supply ships, but this was often augmented by game, including ptarmigan, Arctic char and a particular delicacy – deer tongues. The Bay men, especially recruits from the Orkneys' rocky shores, were offered daily fare far better than they might have had at home.

The prodigious consumption of food was easily matched by the quaffing of great volumes of alcohol. The Company quickly realized that liquor was as great a danger to its trade as the climate, but no matter how many prohibitions it proclaimed or how often

Paddlers wearing veils to shield them from the swarms of mosquitoes that had so plagued James Knight.

it paid off informers to halt the smuggling of brandy casks on outgoing ships, the booze flowed steadily across the Atlantic.

With kegs of "brandy" (cheap gin, in fact, coloured to look like brandy) required for the Indian trade, the Company was forced to institute regular rations (one quart each Wednesday and Saturday) for its own personnel. According to account books from Prince of Wales's Fort, by 1721 each Bay man averaged seven and a half gallons of brandy a year. Because several were teetotallers, the actual amount the drinkers put away was probably closer to ten gallons each – and that didn't include the illicit trade.

Factors complained about "the sots" they had been assigned and urged the Committeemen to recruit fresh-faced country lads "not debauched by the voluptuousness of London." But even these rural innocents quickly learned that interminable months in a dark, cold cabin made alcohol a virtual tonic for survival.

And so the Company men, perched on the desolate perimeter of Hudson Bay, were suffocated by inertia for the first half of the eighteenth century. The slowly revolving cycle of the fur trade – the spring and autumn goose hunts, the ptarmigan and rabbit shoots in winter, freeze-up and breakup, the summer curse of the mosquitoes, the annual arrival and departure of the supply ships – these and other minor interruptions only rarely disturbed what was otherwise a dreary survival mode, fostering from one generation to the next not only a fixed sense of place but a rigid state of mind. The Bay men kept their thoughts focused homeward, as if unexplored regions to the back of them were occupied by the land equivalents of allegorical creatures in the "Here Be Dragons" admonitions of early chartmakers. A 1782 map of North America, published in London by Thomas Conder, depicted all the land west of Hudson Bay as a blank, with the notation: "These parts intirely unknown."

Apart from a 1686 journey to the mouth of the Churchill River from York Factory by two HBC captains, John Abraham and Michael Grimington, only the travels into buffalo country of the boy explorer Henry Kelsey four years later and the doomed dash northward by James Knight in 1719 disrupted the bay-bound isolation.

Kelsey is now hailed as "The Discoverer of the Canadian Prairies" or summarily dismissed by historians such as Lawrence Burpee, who concluded that his narrative was "too unsubstantial to afford any safe ground for historical conclusions." Kelsey would later in his career become one of the HBC's senior overseas supervisors, spending nearly forty years in a faithful, if prosaic, anticlimax to his 1690 mission. (continued on page 64)

Supply ships leaving Gravesend. These annual expeditions provided the only contact between the isolated Bay posts and the outside world.

LIFE BY THE FROZEN SEA

"Nine months of winter, varied by three of rain and mosquitoes" is how a chief factor in the 1840s described the climate at York Factory. For the men who staffed the Bay's outposts life was a dreary routine in an unrelenting environment.

Food and drink provided the main solaces amid the monotony and isolation. Provisions of salted meats, cheese, flour, oatmeal, butter and other staples brought over on supply ships were supplemented

(Right) Each HBC post had a bachelors' hall like this one at Norway House, where card and dice games and holiday revels and dancing (above) took place.

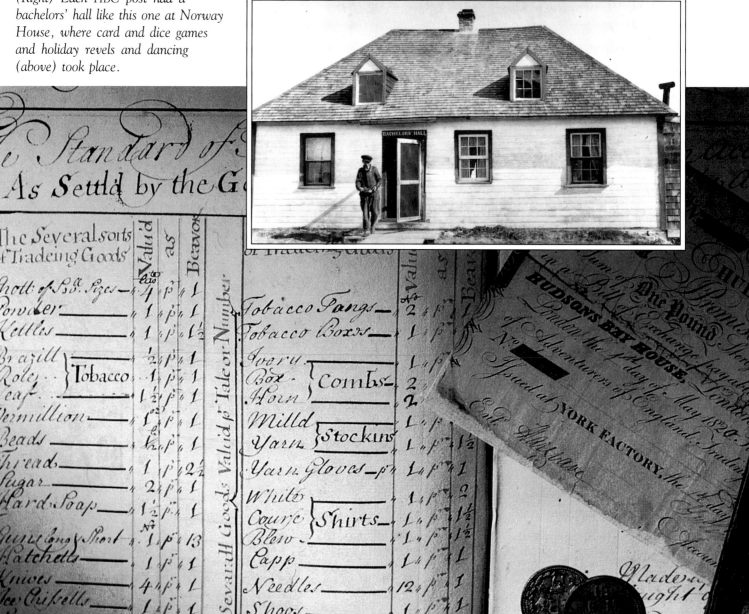

by locally shot game and birds. Although the daily fare was superior to what many of the men would have eaten at home, food was sometimes a source of discontent, particularly since many delicacies were reserved for the Factor's table.

But the main cure for cabin fever was provided by alcohol. As early as 1682, the HBC had shipped 440 gallons of brandy to its posts and it was the rare Company servant who did not have his own cache of private stock. During the riotous Christmas week celebrations at York Factory in 1861, an appalled observer noted that 104 gallons of liquor had been consumed by a population of fifty.

(Opposite, bottom) Meticulous ledger-keeping was a daily activity for Company clerks. Wooden tokens aided factors in explaining mathematics while brass tokens represented beaver. HBC pound notes were legal tender in Company territories.
(Left, top) Light streams into the shuttered interior of the Anglican chapel at York Factory where pew seating was once rigidly assigned in order of hierarchy at the post.
(Left, bottom) Bay men at York Factory during the 1800s prepare for the arrival of a supply ship.
(Below) The graves of those who never returned from the frozen shore, the headstones heaved by permafrost.

TRADE GOODS

The beaver had drawn the gentleman adventurers to the shores of Hudson Bay in the first place and beaver pelts soon became the standard measure for doing business, specifically what the traders referred to as "made" beaver — meaning one good-quality pelt from an adult animal. Other forms of fur were quoted in their beaver equivalents (two otter skins were worth one made beaver, a moose skin, two, for instance) and the prices of all goods traded by the Company were in made beaver. Company records from Albany Fort in 1733 give the following rates of exchange: a single made beaver pelt could be traded for either a brass kettle, two pounds of Brazil tobacco or twenty steel

(Right) An Indian barters furs for a flintlock in artist C.W. Jefferys's impression of an eighteenth century trading post.
(Below) A Hudson's Bay blanket with its distinctive multi-coloured stripes.

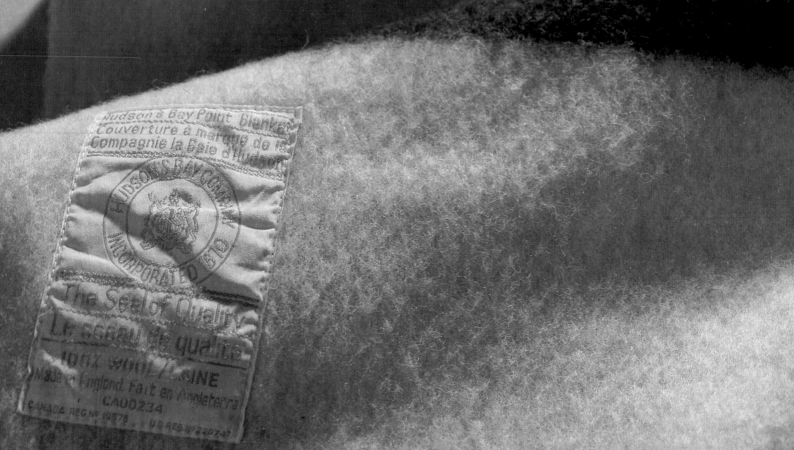

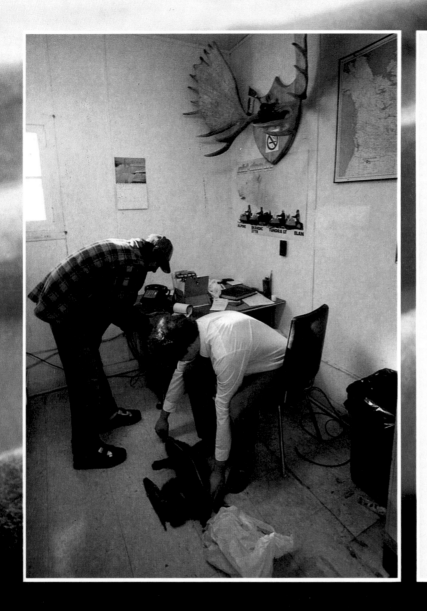

fish-hooks. To avoid alienating their fur-gathering clientele, the Company did not alter these prices much over time, even as the price of beaver furs fell in Europe. There could, however, be fluctuations in the cost of some items from post to post.

The most sought-after beaver pelts were those worn by the natives themselves, where regular use had loosened the outer coating of fur, making them ideal for felt-making. The Hudson's Bay blanket, the most durable legacy of the Company's involvement in the fur trade, was developed so that Indians could trade "the very furs off their backs" and still have something warm to wear on their way home. Introduced at the end of the eighteenth century, the blanket's trademark coloured stripes were added later on, and the modern blanket still bears a set of small

(Left) A modern-day Hudson's Bay Company clerk examines a fur brought in by a customer at the Company store near Little Grand Rapids on Lake Winnipeg.

black stripes along its edge representing the number of made beaver pelts that size of blanket was worth. Hudson's Bay blankets were often cut into coats and leggings, their snowy colour allowing a hunter to blend in with the winter landscape.

A persistent myth of the fur trade concerns the number of beaver pelts required in trade for a rifle. The story has it that the Company demanded a pile of made beaver pelts equal in height to the length of the gun when stood on its end. Then, in an act of capricious cruelty, the Company started making the gun barrels longer and longer, requiring more and more furs.

The story is apocryphal. HBC guns did not grow longer with time. For nearly two centuries, from 1700 to the late 1800s, the Company sold guns in standard lengths of 36, 42 or 48 inches. Nor was the cost calculated against the gun's length, which in the case of the longest guns would have required a pile of furs five feet high and consisting of about three hundred pelts. The common price in furs for a rifle was about a dozen made beaver, give or take a pelt or two.

For the most part, it was in the Company's own interests to deal fairly with their customers, to offer products that were of practical use. Only later, when the HBC faced increased competition from French pedlars did this policy change. Then, the Company altered its emphasis from immediately practical goods to one which would have a profoundly negative effect on its customers: alcohol.

Above) François Gros Louis, a nineteenth-century Indian trapper, is a virtual walking advertisement for HBC trade goods. His clay pipe is of a kind offered by the Company, as is the trap at his side. His rifle, here carried across his shoulder and wrapped in fur, was probably also obtained in trade from an HBC post.

(Opposite) Arranged atop the furs they would have been purchased with are various Company trade goods from the eighteenth and nineteenth centuries. They are (1) musket balls and a powder horn, (2) coloured beads, (3) knife blades, (4) a flint-lock rifle, (5) clay pipes for smoking the Company's excellent Brazil tobacco, another popular trade good, (6) copper wire, used in making snares, (7) copper cooking pots in a variety of sizes, (8) a steel leghold trap and (9) a Hudson's Bay blanket, an item still in demand today.

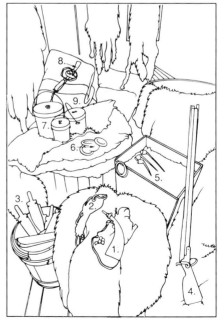

He was sent not on a voyage of exploration but "to call, encourage and invite the remoter Indians" to bring their furs eastward to the bay. North America's first travelling salesman, he carried a packet of trade supplies: Brazil tobacco, glass beads, hatchets and kettles. Heading southwest from York Factory, he reached a sheltered bend in the Saskatchewan River below what is now The Pas, Manitoba, and after successfully wintering there continued westward into the Assiniboine country, reaching the buffalo-rich Touchwood Hills southeast of present-day Saskatoon. Kelsey's two-year foray was rich in new experience; he rode with the Indians on bison hunts, was the first white man to view the Prairies, and he arrived back at York Factory at the head of a "good fleet of Indians." Yet, judging by the lack of any follow-up to his travels, his journey might as well have never happened.

A significant but mysterious figure in the roster of Bay men who risked themselves on the land's illusory mercies, James Knight spent four eventful decades in the Company's service. Originally apprenticed as a shipwright at Deptford, he joined the HBC in 1676 as a staff carpenter. The energetic Knight proved himself so capable that only six years later he was named Chief Factor at Albany. After his return to England, he was accused of private trading in furs and was dismissed – but only briefly. When Albany Post was captured by the French, the Company needed an attack flotilla to get it back, and Knight was rehired to lead the expedition. Sailing off in June 1692 with a four-ship convoy and 213 men, the most formidable expedition the Company itself ever sent into the bay, Knight's troops quickly took the almost-abandoned Albany. When he returned to England five years later, Knight was wealthy enough to acquire £400 in HBC stock.

That purchase, plus his practical experience, was recognized in 1711 when Knight became one of the very few overseas Bay men to be honoured with a seat on the London Committee.

Knight realized that with a trading post built only seven days' paddling up the Albany River, the French and their Huron and Algonquin allies were hemming in the HBC posts with increasingly effective competition, siphoning off the flow of prime furs. Since the HBC did not have enough men or arms to force a confrontation, Knight decided to try outflanking "the woodrunners" by seeking new fur-trading grounds to the north, out of reach of their Montreal-based routes. An expedition, led by William Stuart, a Company servant only semi-literate in English but fluently articulate in Cree, was sent to make contact with the inland Chipewyan. Stuart not only achieved this goal, but his inland journey pushed into brief prominence one of the most striking personalities of the

(Opposite) On his journey inland, Kelsey became the first Bay man to see the Prairies.

early Canadian fur trade: Thanadelthur. A Chipewyan by birth, she had been captured by the Cree as a teenager, then escaped and made her way to Ten-Shilling Creek near York Factory. Appointed as Stuart's interpreter by James Knight, whom she had impressed, the success of Stuart's expedition was due in large part to Thanadelthur's role in mediating between the hostile Cree and Chipewyan. Thanadelthur also taught herself English and began to spin into Knight's attentive ear alluring tales of rich mineral deposits. Like many Bay men since Prince Rupert, he had long dreamed of such an El Dorado and had prudently brought with him from England "Cruseables, melting potts, borax &c., for the Trial of Minerals." Thanadelthur's promise to lead Knight to the mineral showings went unfulfilled, however, for she fell ill and died on February 5, 1717.

Before her death, Thanadelthur had described to Knight a broad strait in her country through which great tides ebbed and flowed, suggesting the existence of the elusive North West Passage. But the HBC veteran was much more enthralled by her tales of "Yellow mettle" and "black pitch" – possible references to Klondike gold and the Athabasca tar sands. Her disjointed narrative had been peppered with vague tales of a lost tribe of bearded white giants gathering bags of gold and mining mountains of copper beyond the northern horizon. The gossip among HBC posts at the time was that "Governor Knight knew the way to the place as well as to his bedside." One group of visiting Chipewyan drew him a rough map of the Copper Indians' country, sketching a specific route to the Coppermine, fourteen river-crossings to the north and west of Churchill. They assured him that just beyond these copper hills lay the Great Western Sea and that inhabitants there had spotted strange vessels, which Knight took to be Japanese or Tartar ships at the western end of the North West Passage.

Hardly able to contain his excitement, the credulous veteran, now in his seventies, hurried back to England in the autumn of 1718 to obtain the Committee's backing for a major voyage of discovery. Persuaded by their elder colleague's faith in the existence of distant lucre, the Committee granted Knight its blessing and the funds to outfit two vessels, the hundred-ton frigate *Albany* and the forty-ton sloop *Discovery*, with a twenty-seven-man crew between them, plus two captains and ten "landsmen passengers."

The Committeemen's instructions contained a highly unusual codicil: Knight's captains were expressly forbidden to land at any Company post on Hudson Bay or even to trade south of latitude 64°north where commercial contact had already been made. This was presumably put in to avoid exacerbating the quarrel between

Thanadelthur making peace between Cree and Chipewyan warriors.

Knight and his York Factory Deputy and eventual successor, Henry Kelsey, the one-time boy explorer. There was strong distrust between the two since Knight had accused Kelsey of conniving with the Indians in the theft of Company goods. The younger and intensely ambitious Kelsey complained he had not been sufficiently recognized by the HBC hierarchy for his historical wilderness trek into the interior; the old Governor, who had held every honour within the Company's grant, felt that he had yet to make any history or earn much of a fortune.

Neither man would attain his goal. Knight was to die in frigid isolation on one of Hudson Bay's bleakest outcrops; Kelsey would be recalled to England under a cloud of unsubstantiated suspicion and vanish from the Company's books with no official mention made of his thirty-eight years of loyal service or his magnificent journey inland.

Although Knight's expedition ranked as one of the most tragic Arctic disasters, no one in London seemed particularly concerned about his fate. Without attempting to resolve the reason for the expedition's disappearance, on September 29, 1722, the Company wrote off the two ships and crews in its books as "being castaway to the northward in Hudson Bay...." It wasn't until forty-eight years later that Joseph Stephens and Samuel Hearne stumbled on the physical remains of the expedition on Marble Island off Rankin Inlet. Hearne found the wreckage of the *Albany* and *Discovery* five fathoms deep in a cove on Marble's stony southeast shore, as well as the ruins of a stone house, an anvil and some muskets. Area natives confirmed that Knight had been driven ashore by a storm and had built a shelter. By the second winter illness had reduced the survivors to only five men. According to watching Eskimos, the last two had expired in abject misery: "Many days after the rest, [they] frequently went to the tip of an adjacent rock, and earnestly looked to the South and East, as if in expectation of some vessels coming to their relief. After continuing there a considerable time together, and nothing appearing, they sat down close together and wept bitterly. At length, one of the two died, and the other's strength was so far exhausted that he fell down and died also, in attempting to dig a grave for his companion."

Knight's disappearance remains one of the Arctic's enduring mysteries. Marble Island is within easy sight of the mainland. Knight's men were reported by their Eskimo observers to be at work lengthening one of their longboats in their first season on Marble Island. Why would they sit out two summers in ever-declining numbers within sight of shore? They were only about four days' sail from the HBC post at Churchill. Why, most curiously,

(Above) Arthur Dobbs. (Top, right) Ships of the expedition that was prompted by Arthur Dobbs's efforts probe Wager Inlet.

were no serious attempts made to find them? Knight's fate is an unexplained exception in the HBC's usually precise dealings with its senior factors. Knight's dismal foray only served to reinforce the Company's determination to sit tight on the frozen coast.

What finally helped shake the Company from its slumber was a determined campaign against the HBC staged by a persistent Irishman named Arthur Dobbs. Dobbs's avowed purpose was to force the Company into an active search for the North West Passage, but this worthy cause was mixed with emphatically commercial impulses. Although the eventual effect of the Dobbs intervention was to force the Company into the exploration that eventually saved its Charter, loyal HBCers two centuries later still dismiss him with the vitriol due a brigand.

Starting with two tenuously connected facts – that the North West Passage had not been found and that the HBC owned most of the land around its eastern entrance – Dobbs concluded that either the Company had kept the existence of the waterway secret for its own commercial reasons or that it had not been discovered because the Adventurers were not adventurous enough. He seized on British expansionist sentiments and built his anti-HBC stand into a national crusade of no mean impact. As noted by his biographer, Desmond Clarke, Dobbs "viewed the Hudson's Bay Company…as a fat, wealthy monopoly sated with profits, and sleeping in inglorious ease while the French increased their power and influence in Northern Canada."

The son of the high sheriff of County Antrim in the north of Ireland, Dobbs multiplied his family wealth by marrying the heiress Anne Osburn and sat in the Irish House of Commons from 1721 to 1730. Tutored in part by a very young Jonathan Swift, then serving as a village parson, Dobbs won appointment to the post of Surveyor-General of Ireland. Doggedly ambitious, he became friendly with Lord Conway, a cousin of Sir Robert Walpole, the

British prime minister. Seeking to widen his influence, Dobbs in 1730 crossed to London, where he was introduced to many of the City's leading functionaries and began advocating resumption of the search for a North West Passage. The HBC's Governor, Sir Bibye Lake, all but ignored Dobbs, humouring him by sending a whaling sloop up the bay's west coast to seek an opening. When that failed, Lake blandly reported the fruitless trip to Dobbs and excused the HBC from further geographical ventures.

Realizing that the Company had been trifling with him, Dobbs spent the next twelve years in the most concentrated attack ever mounted against the HBC. Dobbs's manoeuvrings eventually resulted in the first Royal Navy expedition to search for the Passage. Under the command of Captain Christopher Middleton, one of the HBC's most experienced supply-ship veterans and a convert to Dobbs's cause, the expedition wintered for a year at Prince of Wales's Fort, then struck out for the Arctic. Middleton probed and named Wager Inlet and sailed to the sandy terminus of Roes Welcome, being so disappointed that it wasn't the Passage he named it Repulse Bay. Having ventured farther north in the bay than any white man before him, Middleton steered his ships home safely, only to be condemned by Dobbs for not pursuing his exploration and accused of having been bribed by the HBC.

Dobbs later organized the North West Committee, which funded an independent expedition into Hudson Bay; it also failed to find a Passage. Undeterred, he argued that since the existence of the Passage had not been disproved, it must therefore exist. He petitioned the King in Council to grant his Committee trading arrangements similar to those of the HBC – in effect demanding precisely the kind of monopoly he had been condemning. At the time, British merchants, especially in the burgeoning ports of Liverpool and Bristol, were attacking the London-based trading monopolies. Seventeen petitions questioning the HBC's Charter eventually reached Parliament, and faced with a growing public outcry, a special committee was struck to hear the complaints. Headed by Lord Strange, the group listened to a litany of criticism inspired by Dobbs and his entourage. The HBC's Governor, Thomas Knapp, who came to office three years after the long tenure of Sir Bibye Lake had ended, did not deign to appear but sent the special committee a stack of documents, including a suddenly resurrected description of Henry Kelsey's epic journey and the log of every ship that had ever stuck its bow north of Churchill. James Isham, Factor at Prince of Wales's Fort, crossed the Atlantic to testify on the Company's behalf, providing a calm rationale for

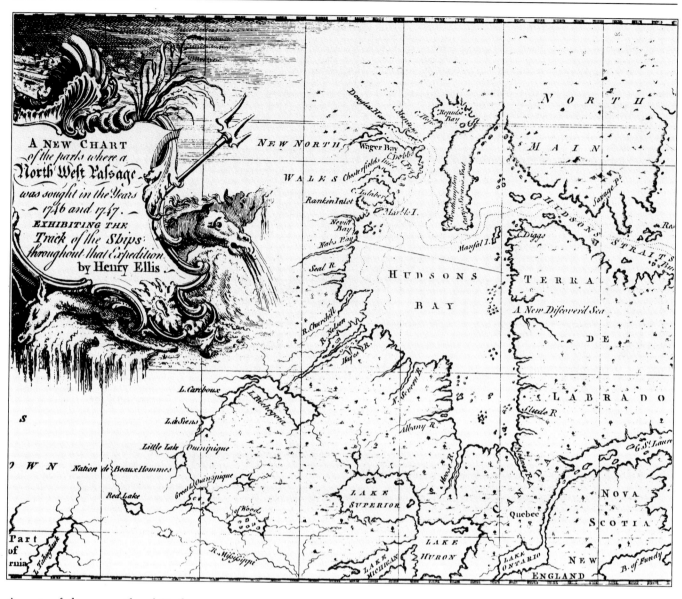

A map of the west side of Hudson Bay based on Middleton's expedition. Despite such evidence, Dobbs remained convinced that the North West Passage existed.

its status-quo policies. Finally, the HBC's solicitor went so far as to pledge a careful move towards expansion.

After hearing twenty-two witnesses, Lord Strange ruled that there was no case for annulling the HBC Charter or interfering with the Company's trade position. The parliamentarians realized that even if Dobbs's mythical passage did exist, it would not be commercially navigable, and that in view of the climate and geography of Hudson Bay, the Company's understandable emphasis on survival could not be dismissed. A disgruntled Dobbs retired to his "rural amusements" in Carrickfergus, Ireland, studying the swarming habits of bees and left the search for the Passage to "some more happy Adventurer." Named Governor of North Carolina in 1754, the pugnacious Irishman died there eleven years later.

A TRAPPER'S LIFE

Whatever its imperial pretensions, the livelihood of the Hudson's Bay Company depended on the skills and motivation of a far-flung network of trappers. For as long as the Company was directly involved in the fur business, it was the trappers who kept the furs flowing into the trading posts, ensuring the Company's financial well-being.

A trapper's life was largely defined by the weather and the natural cycles of the animals he hunted. It was a hard existence and remains so today, even though technological advances have reduced some of the challenges. Since the advent of the steel trap in the early nineteenth century, hunters have been freed from having to pursue their quarry. In the case of the beaver, the steel trap meant that, instead of having to lie in wait with an ice chisel lashed to a stick until one of the creatures appeared, one could set a trap baited with castoreum, a gooey substance taken from a beaver's perineal glands. In recent years, the snowmobile has also made life immeasurably easier for the trapper.

There are still, however, individuals who lead lives similar to those of trappers one hundred and fifty years ago. Pi Kennedy, a Cree Indian from the Northwest Territories, is one of them. Few men are as self-sufficient as Kennedy, who works and lives alone while on the trapline, with only his dogs for company. Kennedy's cabin is about a day-and-a-half's journey from Fort

(Above, right) Pi Kennedy checks one of the snares on his trapline. Essentially a noose made out of copper wire, the snare can be used to catch wolf, coyote, fox or lynx. Opponents of such traps decry the suffering they say they cause.

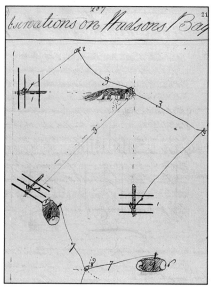

A 1743 sketch of an elaborate trap consisting of a trip wire connected to a gun.

A snare in place on Pi Kennedy's trapline.

Smith, where he sells his furs. Kennedy is constantly on the move. When he isn't tending his dogs, which he feeds fish he has caught near his cabin or the occasional moose he has been lucky enough to bag, he is walking his trapline to check his snares or preparing traps to place underwater near a beaver lodge on a frozen lake. Kennedy must check these

(Right) Pi Kennedy outside his cabin with a beaver pelt.
(Below) Washing after a day on the trapline. In the wilderness, bathing is a luxury.

traps daily, or else they will become hopelessly frozen under the lake. Another of his tasks is chopping trees for firewood, which he burns in his cabin stove, his sole source of heat and comfort. At night, the glow cast by his fire and his lamp on the snows outside his windows is the only indication of human habitation for many miles around.

(Left) A nineteenth-century picture of a trapper, his wife and their dogsled. (Below) Pi Kennedy on his dogsled. Most trappers now prefer to travel by snowmobile.

CHAPTER FIVE

THE PATHFINDERS

THE PARLIAMENTARY HEARINGS HEADED BY LORD STRANGE had made the Company the focus of unprecedented and unwelcome publicity. To the dismay of the London Committeemen, their shareholder lists, business methods, reluctant exploration policies and even their profit margins had become the subject of public debate. It became clear that the much-vaunted Charter of 1670 could prove to be no more than a scrap of parchment. Royally chartered companies had by the mid-eighteenth century begun to seem anachronistic, and Parliament was already demanding that the Company define the limits of its territories.

Faced with this evolution in the business climate, the HBC, as it would so often throughout its history, roused itself from complacency: it authorized a probe into the interior from York Factory to "draw down many of the natives to trade." The trek was undertaken by a former smuggler named Anthony Henday employed by the HBC as a net-mender. No other journey from the shoreside posts had been officially sanctioned by the Company since Henry Kelsey's return from his meandering westward probe half a century earlier.

Henday's mission, though triggered by the Dobbs affair, had other more urgent promptings. Hudson's Bay Company traders had long heard grim warnings of French incursions into the fur-rich hinterland. Nearly a quarter century earlier, Pierre Gaultier de Varennes, Sieur de La Vérendrye, and his sons had begun to set down the matrix of Montreal's future inland trade, and by 1754 these "woodrunners" occupied many of the traditional canoe routes to Hudson Bay, slashing the HBC's annual fur harvest.

Henday saw for himself the extent of the French trade when, four months out from York Factory, he stood on a patch of bald prairie near the present site of Edmonton. This was no wilderness panorama, for Henday was watching busy French traders loading their canoes. "I don't very well like it," he recorded apprehensively in his journal. "Having nothing to satisfy them on what account I

(Opposite) Anthony Henday entering the Blackfoot camp in 1754.

am going up the country and very possably [sic] they may expect me to be a spy...."

His competitors left him alone, mainly because he was accompanied by a large troop of Indians led by a Cree named Attickasish who, Henday noted, "has the charge of me." His constant companion was a Cree woman who acted as his food gatherer and cook and was officially listed as his interpreter, though Henday referred to her in the version of his journal not sent to London as "my bed-fellow."

On October 1, 1754, seven stern hunters dressed in bison skins and armed with bone-tipped spears rode into Henday's camp, located southeast of present-day Red Deer, Alberta. They were Bloods from the powerful Blackfoot Confederacy that reigned supreme in the Western Prairie and controlled the approaches to the mysterious foothill country. After much preliminary prying, they escorted Henday to their main camp, a portable city of more than two hundred painted tepees pitched in two long rows. The encampment was abuzz with excitement as the white man was led to the great meeting hall, a buffalo-hide lodge that could seat fifty elders. Sweetgrass smoke was wafted about and the traditional calumets were passed hand to hand in a hush as the rulers of the plains quizzically examined the stranger from the shores of the inland sea. Boiled buffalo meat was served in baskets of woven grass and the gift of a dozen buffalo tongues, the tastiest of local delicacies, was formally presented to Henday. But when the visitor began to bargain with the Blackfoot chief to send some of his men back with him, Henday was rebuffed first by silence and later with the sensible explanation that the Blackfoot would not leave their horses or abandon the buffalo hunt, that they did not know how to use canoes and had heard of many Indians starving on their way to Hudson Bay.

The Henday expedition pushed farther west, reaching the site of Innisfail, Alberta, less than forty miles from where Rocky Mountain House, the famous trading post, would arise. The geographical co-ordinates of Henday's westernmost location – 51°50'N, 114°W – placed him within clear view of the Rocky Mountains, but his journal is oddly silent on his reaction to such a dramatic sighting. Like every other explorer of his day, Henday hoped to discover the western sea – not a massive rock barrier. Facing the immensity of the Rocky Mountains, which stretched toward the horizon like a continent unto themselves, he may have chosen to deny their existence. "The water very salt, smells like Brine," he scribbled in his journal while tramping through the rolling western parkland.

On the return journey, his accompanying flotilla sometimes swelling to sixty canoes, Henday realized that the Cree were so well established as fur-trade middlemen that they would not permit interior Indians to undertake the long Hudson Bay journey themselves. Documentation of that proposition, which would eventually prompt the HBC to appreciate the complexities of the inter-tribal trading patterns, was the most valuable contribution of Henday's mission. That and his report about the sophistication of the French traders at Fort Pasquia, a post near The Pas that had been established by La Vérendrye: "The French talk several languages to perfection; they have the advantage of us in every shape, and if they had Brazile tobacco would entirely cut our trade off." Significantly, Henday's own Cree companions twice traded their furs to the French for brandy.

When the salute guns boomed York Factory's welcome on June 23, 1755, Henday had been away for a year. Chief Factor James Isham questioned the traveller closely and suggested to London that the HBC dispatch several men inland with roving commissions to bring the Indians out to trade and "root the French out."

Rival fur traders are shown racing towards an Indian camp in this print by Frederic Remington.

But in the autumn of 1755, even as Henday was sailing home out of Hudson Bay, other developments in other arenas all but obliterated the memory of his exploits. The Royal Navy was already at sea with the orders to intercept supplies from France for its North American colonies. Without any formal declaration, the Seven Years' War had begun. The subsequent surrender of Quebec in 1759 convinced the London Committeemen that the golden age of their monopoly had finally dawned; they (wrongly) assumed that the "woodrunners" would somehow vanish and leave all the fur revenues to them. Yet by 1764, charter or no charter, the western trading routes were once again crowded with Montreal canoes. As historian Glyndwr Williams observed, "The Charter was no longer attacked – it was simply ignored by the traders who inherited the old French routes west from Montreal and pushed on towards the Pacific." The Montreal-based "pedlars" insisted that the part of Rupert's Land in which they travelled and traded belonged to the French king's domains and was thus not subject to the HBC document which specifically excluded the lands of "any other Christian Prince."

Yet it was not this renewed threat to Company trade that spurred the Committeemen to order a further inland trek, but revived rumours of mineral wealth in the north country.

When Moses Norton, Governor at Prince of Wales's Fort, plunked down a chunk of rich copper ore on the polished mahogany Committee-room table, reporting that the metal had recently been brought out of the north by two Chipewyan, the impatient London directors ordered Norton to mount an expedition "far to the north, to promote an extension of our trade, as well as for the discovery of a North West Passage (and) Copper Mines…taking observation for determining the longitude and latitude, and also distances, and the course of rivers and their depths." The man picked to lead the expedition was an enthusiastic young sailor named Samuel Hearne.

Hearne had grown up in England's capital, where his father was secretary of the London Bridge Water Works Company, and had joined the Royal Navy at the age of twelve, spending half a dozen years at sea. When the Seven Years' War ended in 1763, Hearne left the Navy and three years later joined the HBC as mate on the little sloop *Churchill*. Five years later, Prince of Wales's Fort, where Hearne spent the winters, received its first distinguished visitor, William Wales, the British astronomer-mathematician dispatched by the Royal Society to observe the transit of Venus across the face of the sun. His stay allowed Hearne to improve his knowledge of surveying and chartmaking. The following spring, Hearne, twenty-four and in full vigour, was distressed at being passed by for a captaincy, having been appointed mate of the *Charlotte* instead. He appealed to London for an assignment a notch more senior.

A portrait of an elegantly attired Samuel Hearne, painted after his return to London in 1787.

Moses Norton's decision to pick Hearne to lead the trek inland was only partly based on the youthful seaman's proven abilities. The two men despised one another, and the best solution was geographical separation. In his posthumously published journal, Hearne described the Prince of Wales's Governor, who had made several local Indian women his mistresses, as "one of the most debauched wretches under the sun…," a man who lived "in open defiance of every law, human and divine." Whatever the state of Norton's disposition, the Governor gave Hearne his opportunity.

Samuel Hearne's three journeys inland took him across the Barren Ground, the plain which sprawls across the top of North America. At its southern edges, in sheltered hollows, gale-blasted evergreens peter out into scatterings of dwarf spruce that take three centuries to grow the height of a man. Northward, the underbrush gives way to a topographical void under featureless skies. A relic of the Pleistocene Epoch, the mainland section of the Barrens rolls on for half a million square miles in a rough upside-down triangle formed by Hudson Bay, the saw-toothed perimeter of the Arctic Ocean and the Mackenzie River system.

To venture across the Barren Ground in Samuel Hearne's time meant stepping off the edge of the known world. Still, the mood was festive as he set off on his first expedition during a pre-dawn snow flurry on November 6, 1769. Accompanied by two Company servants and a pair of Cree hunters from Prince of Wales's Fort, he left at the same time as a group of Chipewyan led by an Indian known as Captain Chawchinahaw. Only three weeks later, two hundred miles north of the fort, Chawchinahaw and his band abruptly plundered Hearne's food stocks, then turned southwest, mockingly suggesting that Hearne and his companions find their own way home. As the Indians decamped, Hearne's survival instinct asserted itself. Deprived of provisions and flintlocks, the survivors set off south, escaping starvation by snaring a few rabbits and gnawing the boiled hide of their jackets. It was a mortifying experience, but by the time Hearne stumbled into his home fort, he had been transformed into a resourceful man-of-the-land.

By February 1770 Hearne was itching to set off again, and Norton this time placed him under the dubious protection of a hired Indian named Conne-e-quese who claimed to have seen the Arctic copper mines. They reached the edge of the Barrens by June, Hearne stumbling along, weighed down by a sixty-pound shoulder sack and his awkward quadrant, his face smeared with goose grease to ward off the swarms of mosquitoes and flies so thick they shadowed the sun. Finding no game to shoot, the party was reduced to munching cranberries or chewing scraps of hide and burned bones from long-abandoned fires. When Hearne reached Yathkyed Lake, deeper into the Barrens than any white man before him, his group was joined by parties of roaming Chipewyan who eventually swelled the aggregation to nearly six hundred. The incompetent Conne-e-quese, no longer certain where he was or even whether the copper outcrops really existed, decided to winter with the nomads. Hearne had no choice but to agree. Shortly afterward, his quadrant was tipped over and broken by a gust of wind as he was setting up a sighting to calculate where he was. Far from his home fort, his few trade goods gone and his companions grumbling about how useless he was, Hearne had his future course decided for him when several of the Indians stole his personal possessions.

The heralding chill of winter was in the air; Hearne was lost and alone. Having nabbed his belongings, the Indians went on their way. Convinced he would soon freeze or starve, Hearne permitted himself a rare note of harsh self-pity, complaining to his journal: "I never saw a set of people that possessed so little humanity, or that could view the distress of their fellow creatures with so little feeling and unconcern...." He had no snowshoes, no tent or warm clothes. He doggedly trudged south for three

This naive European image of an Eskimo was drawn at approximately the same time as Hearne's journey to the Coppermine River.

days, falling asleep later and later each night to try to hold off the moment when his willpower would evaporate and he would welcome delirium, surrendering himself to the long Arctic slumber from which there is no waking.

Then occurred one of those theatrical events that characterize the Hudson's Bay chronicles. On September 20, 1770, just a day before Hearne would almost certainly have frozen to death, there materialized out of the void a tall, dark apparition – Matonabbee, greatest of the Chipewyan chiefs. For the first time, Samuel Hearne was facing his mentor and soulmate. The two men would through the years forge a unique partnership of mutual admiration and even love. Hearne praised Matonabbee for his "scrupulous adherence to truth and honesty that would have done honour to the most enlightened and devout Christian," describing his personality as combining "the vivacity of a Frenchman and the sincerity of an Englishman with the gravity and nobleness of a Turk."

A handsome six-footer with a hawk nose and brooding eyes, Matonabbee had been born at Prince of Wales's Fort, the son of a Cree slave-girl and a local Chipewyan hunter. Adopted by Richard Norton (Moses's father), the young Matonabbee learned to speak Cree as well as some English, and taught himself the workings of the fur trade. He was probably the only Chipewyan of his time who felt at home both on the Barrens and inside the HBC forts.

And so Matonabbee plucked Hearne from the shores of eternity, provided him with otter robes, directed him to woods where they could make snowshoes and sleds, then guided him back to Prince of Wales's Fort. The two men agreed en route to strike out for the Coppermine River together and, only twelve days after his return from his second journey, Hearne slipped silently out of the Company post. This time he attached himself to Matonabbee and his accompanying retinue of up to eight wives and nine children, in effect becoming a member of that extended family.

This was a most unusual arrangement for its time. Englishmen simply did not subordinate themselves to natives they still described as "red savages." Hearne gave himself up to the natural rhythms and diet of the Barrens while entrusting the success of his mission and his personal safety to Matonabbee. His final (and successful) Coppermine journey, which lasted nineteen months, reconciled Hearne to melding into the nomadic bands of accompanying Indians so effectively that he nearly became one of them.

It took Matonabbee and Hearne four months to reach the Thelewey-aza-yeth River, where tent poles were cut, meat was dried and birch bark collected for making portage-fording canoes before the plunge northward into wild Slave country. At

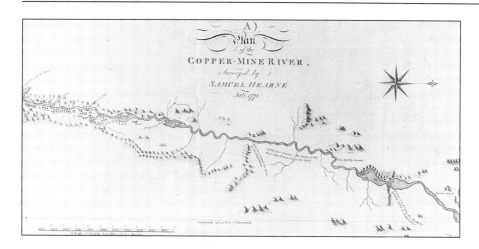

Hearne's map of his expedition to the mouth of the Coppermine River.

times they were accompanying an unruly mob of as many as sixty Chipewyan, and though he displayed the same pragmatic stoicism as his companions, Hearne never lost sight of his personal objectives. They were a ragged little army following their stomachs, their timing and direction dependent on the migrating caribou. Hearne tagged along with his precious journal, lugging a thirty-year-old Elton quadrant and trying to puzzle out exactly where he was. At Clowey Lake, Hearne's party was joined by a foraging band of evasive Indians who refused to explain their mission.

The caravan slanted north and west, dropping most of the wives and children at a camp near Kathawachaga Lake ("Conge-cathawachaga" in Hearne's diary) while preparations went on for the final dash towards the Arctic Ocean. The strangers who had integrated themselves with the main convoy now made for themselves inch-thick wooden shields, carved and painted with spirit symbols Hearne recognized as having nothing to do with hunting. He gradually realized that the newcomers – Copper Indians from the east – were taking over direction of the expedition and that their purpose was to massacre Eskimos known to be frequenting the Coppermine River.

The traditional enmity between Indians and Eskimos has survived into the twentieth century even though no one seems certain how it started. One explanation is that of Dr Robert McGhee, an archaeologist with the National Museum of Civilization, who has postulated that "their mutual hostility can be best understood within the context of Indian hostility against other Indian groups, Inuit against other Inuit – the hostility between most neighbouring groups living in tribal societies...."

The war party sped north, covering eighty rough miles in four days, and crossed the Coppermine River at Sandstone Rapids, about forty miles south of Coronation Gulf. This was the shank of the 1771 summer season, yet on July 3, a raging snowstorm obliterated their tracks. Huddling in the lee of boulders, the warriors shivered in the teeth of the blizzard and dreamed of their triumphs. Scouts sent ahead found the quarry and reported that an Eskimo hunting camp of five tents had been set up at a cataract of the river which Hearne would later appropriately christen Bloody Fall. At this news the Chipewyan tensed, then set about painting their faces, tying up their hair, removing their leggings and finally stripping down to their breechcloths. Gliding silently from stone to stone, they crept along the riverbank. Hearne had been told to stay behind but, nervous that he might be killed by one of the escaping Eskimos, he followed along armed with a spear.

In the summer light just after midnight on July 17 the massacre began. The Indians slithered right up to the tents and hurled themselves at the sleeping Eskimos. The scene was more reminiscent of an abattoir than of a battle, with the panic-stricken victims rearing out of their cozy tents and being impaled on out-thrust spears. More than twenty men, women and children, their faces still sweet from interrupted slumber, were slain within minutes, their death rattles despoiling the Arctic silence. A young Eskimo woman ran desperately towards Hearne, the only man not engaged in the killing. A Chipewyan wheeled and plunged a spear into her side. "She fell down at my feet," Hearne wrote later, "and twisted around my legs, so that it was with difficulty I could disengage myself from her dying grasps. Two Indian men were pursuing this unfortunate victim, and I solicited very hard for her life. The murderers made no reply until they had stuck both their spears through her body and transfixed her to the ground...."

The aftermath was even worse. Hearne mercifully leaves out the details from his journal, remarking only that "the brutish manner in which these savages used the bodies that had been so cruelly bereaved of life was so shocking that it would be indecent to describe it...." The killing stopped but the plunder continued. Their blood-lust played out, the Chipewyan destroyed all evidence of the Eskimos' very existence, hurling their tent poles into the river, even though they might well have been useful. Then the satiated victors sat down for a feast of fresh char.

Within the hour the marauders reverted to being stoic explorers, hiking the eight miles from Bloody Fall to the Arctic Ocean, which Hearne reached at the western end of Coronation Gulf. Here was the destination of all his efforts: journey's end, the ocean he had spent so many months trying to reach. Still caught up in the horror of the murders, he stood transfixed in disappointment by what he saw—a waddle of seals on a nearby floe and a flight of curlew wheeling over the sterile marshland. Nothing else. This

(Opposite) A signature carved by Hearne more than 200 years ago is still clearly visible on a rock near Churchill, Manitoba.

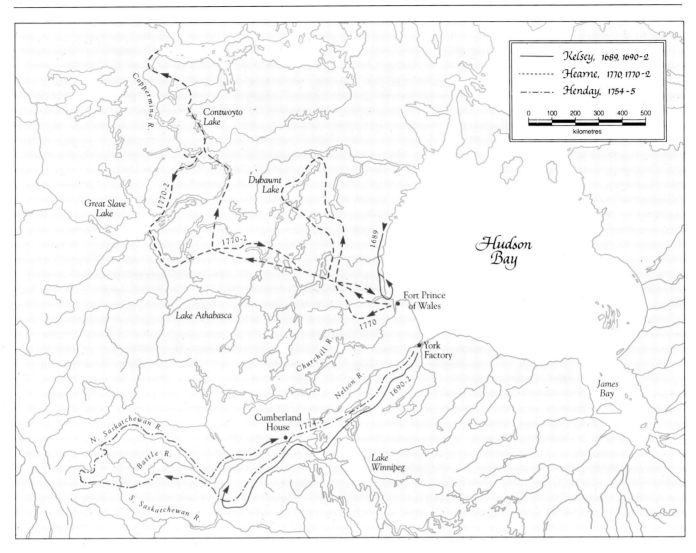

The exploration routes of Henday, Hearne and Kelsey.

was no North West Passage; it was a rocky suburb of Hell. The fabled Coppermine, its mouth nearly blocked by a ridge and impassable shoals, would never accommodate Company ships.

It was one o'clock on the bright morning of July 18, 1771, and the dream of finding a channel across North America had just ended. Men would cast themselves into the quest for another one hundred and thirty-five years, but no one would ever equal Hearne's walk.

Hearne snapped out of his daze and, being a good Company man, did the only sensible thing: "erected a mark, and took possession of the coast on behalf of the HBC."

On the way back, three days' march up the Coppermine then east across Burnt Creek past the September Mountains, Hearne was guided by Matonabbee to the Copper Hills that garnished so many Indian legends. After a four-hour search they found one sizeable chunk of loose metal, a four-pound lump the shape of "an Alpine hare couchant." There was evidence that ore had been taken out of the ground, but with winter coming and the

Chipewyan impatient to be back with their women, Hearne had little time for mineralogy.

The Indians tramped flat out back to their family camp, and for the first time Hearne began to lag behind, his feet punctured by gravel that ate into his flesh, his toenails peeling away. Each step left a footprint of blood. Hearne's return journey spanned nearly another year, partly across a frozen Great Slave – the world's eleventh-largest lake, three hundred miles long and two thousand feet deep. On June 29, 1772, eighteen months and twenty-two days after he had left Prince of Wales's Fort, Hearne reached a familiar spot only ten miles from the fort. In the hunter's way, he settled in to savour one last wilderness camp, planning to make the most of his entrance the following morning. As he sat by the feeble embers of the campfire, he scratched a final triumphant entry into his travel journal: "Though my discoveries are not likely to prove of any material advantage to the Nation at large," he wrote, "or indeed to the Hudson's Bay Company, yet I have the pleasure to think that I have fully complied with the orders of my Masters, and that it has put a final end to all disputes concerning a North West Passage through Hudson's Bay."

Hearne's odyssey has rarely if ever been matched. His round trip of about 3,500 miles, the equivalent of the distance as the crow flies from Gibraltar to Moscow, or Quebec City to Juneau, Alaska, was an epic adventure. This intrepid naif had been the first white man to reach the Arctic Ocean by land, discovering en route Great Slave Lake and the Mackenzie River system and pioneering a new technique for exploration – "going native."

The Company responded to Hearne's magnificent achievement in its customary cavalier style. He was paid a £200 bonus and promptly posted back to his former job as mate of the *Charlotte*. But his exploits were not lost on the London governors: he had come to their notice not merely as a promising neophyte but as a dependable explorer ready for other assignments.

When Hearne again marched inland, in 1774, it was to brave a very different challenge – this time far to the southwest. Montreal traders, by now monopolizing the fur traffic of the Saskatchewan River area, were poised to cut off the Company from its main supply of furs. Hearne was sent to establish Cumberland House, the HBC's first permanent western inland settlement, and to claim Prince Rupert's empire before all was lost.

Hearne sketched this view of Lake Athabasca on his return trek from the Arctic Ocean.

INDIANS
AND THE HBC

The arrival of Company ships on the shores of Hudson Bay had a profound effect on the native inhabitants of the Fur Country. At first glance, the influence of the HBC may seem to have been largely positive. Overnight the local natives were transported from the Stone to the Iron Age, their lives made easier in a hundred little ways. Now they had steel fish-hooks instead of having to depend on carved beaver's teeth, and copper pots for cooking rather than birchbark cauldrons. The Indians who lived along Hudson Bay benefited in another way, too, by becoming middlemen between the

(Above) A Chipewyan family on the shores of Hudson Bay in the early nineteenth century. (Right) Rock paintings near Norway House in northern Manitoba. Painted by Indians five hundred years before the arrival of the white man, the large image is commonly interpreted as a boat or canoe paddled by totemic animals, beavers among them.

Company and other tribes sprinkled across the northern interior of North America. But with such improvements came other changes that were not so beneficial. As the fur trade intensified, the native bands involved began to shift from hunting for survival to hunting for the Bay, killing far more animals than they needed for their own purposes. The Indians were slowly transformed into indentured servants who, in hard times, became highly dependent upon their employer for survival.

Far worse, as competition between the French and English traders intensified, alcohol became an increasingly important trade good. Canadians have traditionally prided themselves on the fact that the battles that took place between the red and white men in the American West did not occur in their own country. But the use of alcohol as a trade good was not much less damaging to the Indians than the U.S. Cavalry. The Hudson's Bay Company, it is true, never sold alcohol to the Indians where the Company held a monopoly over the fur trade, believing that drunken Indians made poor trappers. But with the increased success of the North West Company, the Hudson's Bay's own interests came to the fore, and it entered the alcohol trade.

The introduction of rum and brandy to a people who had no history with alcohol, and no customs governing its use, had predictably catastrophic results: families fell apart and social constraints collapsed in the face of this strange new addiction.

The Company and its competitors had not set out to destroy the Indians. But their presence, and whole-hearted pursuit of their self-interest, reduced the first residents of the Fur Country to an abject level by the middle of the nineteenth century. White men's diseases also played a role. So bad were the effects of the fur trade on the Indians that some tribes in the Fur Country, among them the Chipewyan, vowed to have no further contact with the white man and retreated into the wilderness.

(Below) A.J. Miller's The Rendezvous *shows trappers trading with Plains Indians.*
(Right) A nineteenth-century newspaper illustration chronicles the disastrous effect alcohol had on the Indians.
(Below, right) Indians outside the trading post at Fort Garry.

CHAPTER SIX

A HOWLING CALL

IN THE SPRING OF 1773 AN HBC BOOKKEEPER NAMED Matthew Cocking returned to York Factory with disturbing news. During a lengthy journey into the interior, this plucky accountant's aide had managed to push as far west as the Eagle Hills, near the present site of North Battleford, Saskatchewan. He had hunted with the Blackfoot there and noticed with surprise the energetic flow of the fur trade. In his precise copper-plate script, he reported seeing brigades of incoming canoes directed by the pedlars from Montreal, canoes loaded to the gunwales with kegs of liquor and packs of trade goods. By striving for control of the fur trade in the centre of the continent, the pedlars were drying up traffic to the bay.

Since Anthony Henday's trek almost twenty years before, there had been a running argument within Company circles about inland posts. Now the threat posed by the Montreal pedlars and the actuarial evidence of a decline in beaver pelts traded at York Factory, plus Cocking's precise account of how the rich fur country could be exploited, spurred the London Committeemen to action.

"Canada" at the time extended only from the Detroit River east to the Gaspé and north of the St Lawrence River to Lac St-Jean. The land beyond the St Lawrence Valley belonged either to the HBC or to nomadic tribes. The HBC had been able to butt heads with the Montreal-based competition in this huge domain by sending emissaries inland to lure the Indians out to Hudson Bay, where they could still obtain the best bargains and the heavyweight goods that the pedlars could not carry. But after 1770 the freelance traders began to form partnerships – temporary coalitions of interests – that allowed them to pursue their business much more aggressively. Just before these annually financed "outfits" consolidated into the North West Company, the HBC interrupted its century-long reverie to establish its first permanent western settlement.

(Opposite) A pedlar making gifts to Indians, as painted by Alfred Jacob Miller.

91

Hearne and a clutch of reluctant Orkneymen set out in the spring of 1774 as passengers in deep-laden canoes with Indians who were returning to their hunting grounds, each boat carrying 180 pounds of Brazil tobacco, pouches of gunpowder, shot and six-gallon kegs of brandy as well as building supplies. Every advantageous trading site Hearne saw along the way was already occupied by pedlars hawking rum, knives, flint, awls and needles.

About sixty miles west of the modern-day location of The Pas, in the evergreen slough of northwestern Manitoba at Pine Island Lake (now Cumberland Lake) in Saskatchewan, Hearne finally found his spot. It was a good choice. Cumberland House was strategically situated at convenient river connections to Lake Winnipeg, the Rockies and the Nor'Westers' route towards the Athabasca country, yet it was only 450 miles (about forty days' paddling time) from its supply base at York Factory; the pedlars, being five months' travel away from Montreal, were at a disadvantage in at least that respect. A low-slung log bunker, thirty-eight by twenty-six feet, with a leaky plank roof and moss as caulking, was eventually completed.

With wood-smoke curling from its makeshift chimney, the first full-fledged inland post of the Hudson's Bay Company opened for business. At breakup time the following spring, Hearne proudly led a fur-burdened flotilla of thirty-two canoes down to York Factory. His mission – initiating business at Cumberland House – had succeeded. During the next half-century, HBC traders would march across the continent, eventually commandeering the vast territory from the Great Lakes to the Pacific. "The Company's success sprang in no small degree from the timely foundation of Cumberland House in 1774," historian Richard Glover pointed out. "Had this step not been taken when it was, the Company's chance of surviving and triumphing in its struggle with its rivals would have been much reduced. The margin by which it survived and won was small enough as things were."

Although Hearne himself was ambitious to push the HBC farther inland, the 1775 supply ship from London brought him a promotion. At the age of thirty he was given command of his former home base at Prince of Wales's Fort. There, during Hearne's first autumn as Governor, his old friend Matonabbee arrived with three hundred Indians and the largest Chipewyan fur haul in a century. The ensuing orgy of gift-giving extended far beyond the trade goods owed for the furs and was without precedent in HBC annals. Hearne dressed his former guide in the full uniform of a captain, completely outfitted all six of his wives and supplied copious quantities of guns, hatchets and bayonets, awls, needles, looking-glasses and handkerchiefs. Not satisfied, Matonabbee started to bargain, brazenly demanding even more and suggesting that next time he might take his business to the "Canadian traders." That such a long-time friend of the HBC, while engaging in the largest single barter up to that time, would threaten to switch loyalties was a dangerous indication of how vulnerable the Hudson Bay trade had become to the incursions of the pedlars.

The next half-decade at Prince of Wales's Fort was the happiest period of Hearne's life. He settled into a state of peaceful domesticity with the beautiful Mary Norton, daughter of the polygamous former governor of Prince of Wales. Their affectionate idyll, however, was brutally interrupted by the last and most improbable attack on Hudson Bay. The revolution in the Thirteen Colonies had evolved, with French assistance, into the War of American Independence. Hostilities between the French and the English continued, culminating in a fierce naval engagement on April 12, 1782, in the West Indies, where a British fleet under Rear-Admiral Lord Hood defeated the French and scattered their twenty-six surviving warships.

Three of these vessels – the seventy-five-gun *Sceptre* and two frigates of thirty-six guns each, the *Astrée* and *Engageante* – were ordered to mount an attack on the fur posts of Hudson Bay. Under the command of Jean François de Galaup, Comte de La Pérouse, the fleet sailed north carrying three hundred marines, two eight-inch mortars, three hundred bombs and four field cannons. La Pérouse later noted in *La Gazette de France* that his main concern after entering Hudson Bay was not with waging war but with navigation through the "large islands of ice, which extended beyond our view...."

After a few days trapped in the ice, the vessels broke free, and La Pérouse reported that, "on the 8th of August in the evening, I saw the colours of Fort Prince of Wales." With less than a month of navigable weather left, he must have looked up at the massive battlements and wondered how he could successfully lay siege to this impressive wilderness apparition. Unlike the wooden palisades of other fur posts, the fort had limestone embrasures up to forty feet thick, and, with forty guns, should have been the continent's most impregnable stronghold. Yet once the fleet arrived, Hearne realized he had no chance of withstanding a siege. Before a shot had been fired, the gates of the "invincible" fortress were thrown open and a white tablecloth run up its flagpole.

La Pérouse and Hearne amicably negotiated the surrender, which was unconditional except that it allowed the English to keep their personal possessions. Hearne's lightning capitulation has puzzled historians but the Royal Navy veteran knew the havoc the vessel's naval cannon could inflict, particularly since he had a garrison of only thirty-eight men to return fire. Hearne seemed more concerned with keeping a proper tally of the pillage than with trying to stop it. His account of the incident includes a meticulous detailing of the furs and other stock carried off by the French, right down to "17,350 Goose Quills."

La Pérouse and his men spiked each cannon, blew up the arches of the bastion's magazines and torched anything that would burn. The great fort, which had taken thirty-eight years to build, took half a day to destroy. It would never be occupied again, its battlements surviving as a bleak monument to man's presumptions about the invulnerability of stone citadels.

The HBC men were herded onto the French ships and the victorious flotilla weighed anchor to sail to its next objective: the fur-rich storehouses at York Factory. York Governor Humphrey Marten denied the French their trophies. Having watched the ships arrive, Marten hurriedly loaded most of the post's furs aboard the HBC supply vessel *Prince Rupert*. On a moonless night she slipped away past the French ships and headed straight for England.

With the nip of winter already in the air, La Pérouse's men destroyed York Factory and readied to sail. Most of the HBC prisoners, including Hearne, were shifted to the Company's sloop *Severn*, which had been anchored off York Factory at the time. When the French cut the little sloop loose for her voyage across the Atlantic, Edward Umfreville, York Factory's second-in-command, noted that La Pérouse's "politeness, humanity and goodness secured him the affection of all the Company's officers." Hearne and the French admiral had become friendly during their brief time together; La Pérouse had read parts of the explorer's journal and was so taken with it that he chivalrously insisted its early publication be the essential precondition of returning it to Hearne.

The London Committeemen seemed only mildly chagrined by the plunder of their main outposts, but for Hearne the losses were far greater. His love, Mary Norton, frightened by the French conquerors, had bolted into the Barren Ground where, unprepared for the harsh life, she soon starved to death among her Indian relations. Another victim was Hearne's Indian saviour, the proud Matonabbee, who had become so closely bonded with the HBC and Hearne himself that with the defeat of the English he hanged himself rather than live in shame.

Haunted by the tragedy, Hearne returned to the bay and went listlessly about trying to re-establish the outpost by erecting a

(continued on page 98)

SAMUEL HEARNE AT FORT PRINCE OF WALES

The stone bastion of Fort Prince of Wales was built over a forty-year span to guard Hudson Bay from French incursion. In 1775, at the age of thirty, Samuel Hearne was given command of the star-shaped fortress.

The seven years that followed were a contented idyll within a dramatic life. His companion in the governor's quarters was the beautiful Mary Norton, a daughter of the tyrannical Moses Norton and one of his six country wives. (continued)

Hearne confided to his journal that she would "have shone with superior lustre in any other country." Together they cultivated a menagerie that included tame lemmings, imported canaries, foxes, eagles, squirrels and several beavers so domesticated that "they answered to their names and followed as a dog would do." The governor's other relaxations included watching Indians fashion

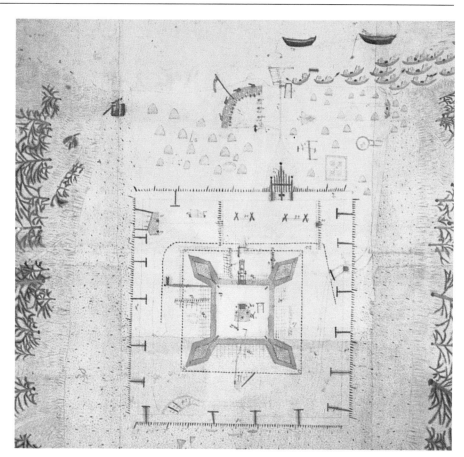

(Previous Page) The only surviving portrait of Hearne shows him as an eighteenth-century dandy rather than the robust wilderness explorer he was. Behind him is an aerial view of Fort Prince of Wales today.
(Right) A rendering by HBC factor James Isham of the plans for the fortress that was to rival France's Louisbourg. (Below) Some of the fort's cannons can still be seen within thick-walled angular bastions.

flutes from the wing-bones of whooping cranes and reading the astringent essays of Voltaire. On August 8, 1782, Hearne surrendered the fort to an invading French force without a shot being fired, bringing down the curtain both on Fort Prince of Wales and the happiest period of his life. The fort that had taken decades to build was destroyed within a few hours. Mary Norton soon died of starvation and Hearne returned to England in 1787, a beaten man.

(Left) A southwest view of Fort Prince of Wales in 1734 from a steel engraving done by Samuel Hearne. (Below) Found on the undersides of boards used as shelves at York Factory, this painting of a factor and his wife at table conveys a scene of domestic comfort in the wilderness similar to that enjoyed by Hearne at Fort Prince of Wales.

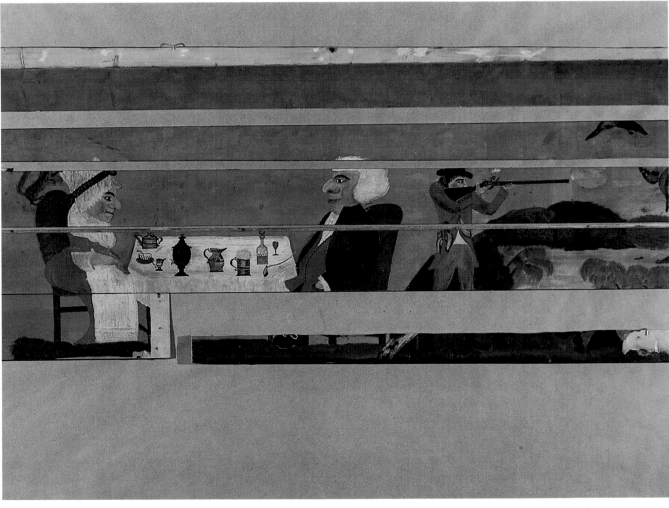

wooden hut five miles upstream from the destroyed fort. But a smallpox epidemic that had spread north from the Mississippi region claimed a staggering toll among the tribes of the Canadian northwest, including nearly half the Chipewyan. Devastated by the epidemic and disillusioned by the HBC's inability to defend its posts, the Chipewyan now seldom emerged from the Barrens. Not surprisingly, the fretful London Committeemen blamed Hearne for the slack in trade. Stung by their criticism and still grieving for his soulmates, Hearne requested home leave. On August 16, 1787, he sailed out of Hudson Bay for the last time, an early victim of the fur trade wars.

The Treaty of Paris (1783) ended the war with the French, but peace did not filter through to the Canadian fur trade. Aided by their mastery of the water routes, the pedlars were now in solid control of the inland fur trade. By 1779, their seasonal, short-term partnerships had been formally amalgamated into the North West Company, dedicated to capturing total control of Canada's fur trade. The continent-wide confrontation between the two fur companies was quickly to become one of the deadliest commercial feuds in history.

The North West Company was the first North American business to operate on a continental scale. Under the direction of the autocratic Scot Simon McTavish – called The Marquis by his partners – its vast holdings were administered with greater efficiency and larger civil budgets than the provinces of Lower and Upper Canada. The NWC's wilderness headquarters, first at Grand Portage and later at Fort William, could accommodate nearly two thousand people at the height of the trading season, its fifteen-foot palisade of pointed timbers enclosing Canada's first inland metropolis.

Beyond the development of a sophisticated trading system that could move furs and trade goods over a precariously overextended transportation network, the most notable feature of this wilderness empire was its roots in original exploration. The true pathfinders and mapmakers of the North American continent's upper latitudes were by and large the fur traders of the North West Company. With a few dramatic exceptions (such as Samuel Hearne and, later, Dr John Rae), the HBC's officers appeared content to remain ensconced around Hudson Bay, prepared to allow others to determine the lay of the land. The Nor'Westers were a more venturesome breed.

Peter Pond, a combative Connecticut Yankee, in 1778 became the first white man to cross the Methy Portage into Athabasca Country. Impressive fur hauls from two seasons in Athabasca re-

Simon McTavish

sulted in Pond's becoming a full partner in one of the first NWC amalgamations. He would return to Athabasca twice more, with an eager neophyte named Alexander Mackenzie serving as his protégé on the final run. Implicated in the murder of two of his competitors, Pond left the Fur Country forever in 1788, and died in poverty in New England, most of his journals used as fuel for kitchen-stove fires.

His understudy, Alexander Mackenzie, was the first European to cross North America north of Mexico. Mackenzie's 1793 feat came thirteen years before Meriwether Lewis and William Clark led a much larger and much better-equipped force to the more southerly American shore of the Pacific. Testing Pond's theory that two broad rivers connected Great Slave Lake north of Lake Athabasca with the Pacific Ocean, Mackenzie set off on the first of his great expeditions from Fort Chipewyan on June 3, 1789. By June 29, he found an entry to the Big River – later to be called the Mackenzie – on Great Slave Lake. The stream initially flowed west, raising Mackenzie's hopes that the Pacific Ocean might appear around one more bend. But then it veered due north. The puny expedition thus lost most of its sense of purpose, and its direction, but the battered canoes meandered down the broad torrent hissing beneath their narrow beams. Finally, in a fog bank at what is now called Garry Island, they landed. That night (July 14, 1789), Mackenzie awakened and sat bolt upright; his belongings were wet from an incoming tide – the conclusive signature of an ocean. After briefly paddling out from the dank coast into the inhospitable Beaufort Sea, Mackenzie and his men hurried southward away from the godforsaken Arctic shore.

By September 12 they were safely back at Fort Chipewyan. They had been gone one hundred and two days, had covered more than three thousand miles and survived unspeakable hardships, only to discover that the Pacific shore they had been seeking must be elsewhere.

Four years later, on May 9, 1793, Mackenzie departed on his greatest adventure. He and his party – an NWC clerk, six voyageurs, two Indians and a large friendly dog – crowded into a specially built twenty-five-foot canoe light enough for two men to portage. By mid-May they were under the brow of the still snow-bound Rockies, passing through the canyons of the Peace River; finally they struck out overland, chopping their way through the brush and forest. Their moccasins were in useless tatters; every footstep was agony. Fearing they would die among the rockslides of these malignant hills, Mackenzie scribbled a note, stuffed it into an empty rum keg and kicked it into the river.

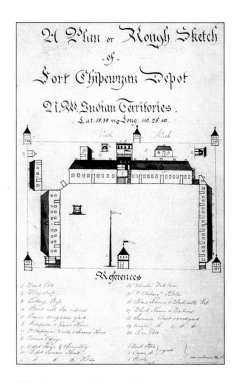

The layout of Fort Chipewyan.

They were near the height of land now, marching silently through the halo of clouds that blotted out the earth except for mountain peaks that appeared to float in these elevated misty seas. Then, unexpected luck. Mackenzie came across a small band of Sekanis, people of the rocks. One of the Indians used a chip of charcoal to sketch the location of a "Great River" that flowed down to what they called a big stinking lake (the Pacific Ocean). Setting out with renewed vigour, the expedition reached two bodies of water, each a source of rivers that flowed in opposite directions. Mackenzie was jubilant: he had reached the Arctic-Pacific divide. All he had to do was to follow the new river to the sea — downstream all the way.

Next day Mackenzie and his men celebrated their good fortune, shooting downstream, their reflexes dulled by their easy passage. Suddenly the canoe was deep in white water exploding into rapids. The frail craft slammed into a rock, almost went over on its port side, was thrown onto a gravel bar and then back into the maelstrom, where its stern was pounded against a boulder. The force of this impact heaved it against the opposite shore and caved in the bow. Trying to steady what was left of their craft, one of the voyageurs grabbed the overhanging branch of a tree, but instead of holding the boat inshore, it catapulted him into the bush. Still somehow floating, the canoe was tossed into a shallow cataract that damaged its bottom, then spewed it out into a calm eddy. Some supplies and many musket balls were lost; the little boat had been reduced almost to kindling.

Next morning they rebuilt their boat and resumed their voyage only to be greeted from the river's shores by a volley of arrows from the Carriers, a fierce tribe who, because of their profitable role as middlemen in the fur business, did not welcome white traders. Mackenzie landed on the opposite shore, beckoning their chief, spreading beads on the ground in a giving gesture. After some hesitation, the Carriers crossed the river in a dugout canoe and the palaver began. Scratching pictures in the mud to make themselves understood, the Carriers told Mackenzie the "Great River" was blocked by cascades that could not be navigated. The Pacific could be reached only by land.

Farther along, Mackenzie and his men cached their canoe as well as much of their food and powder, then set off westward on foot along a trail to the north of the West Road River. With the help of guides, the Nor'Westers crossed the coastal range and entered the wild green rain forest of the Pacific. Welcomed by local Bella Coola Indians who lived in a highly developed, salmon-dependent culture, the explorers were feasted; their hosts even lent them a replacement canoe for the final dash to the ocean. The next day, with the tang of salt in the air, Mackenzie set out to taste the ocean. They reached King Island at the top of Fitz Hugh Sound and were confronted by three canoes of Bella Bellas, hostile natives who threatened Mackenzie's crew. The explorer abandoned the coast but not before making his best-remembered statement. On the southeast face of a large rock the proud Highlander used a mixture of vermilion and bear grease to daub, in large letters, the laconic summary of his incredible journey:

ALEX. MACKENZIE

FROM CANADA

BY LAND

22d JULY 1793

Next morning the party started home and, thirty-three days later, having covered 2,811 miles, they were back at Fort Chipewyan.

For a full decade and a half after Mackenzie's magnificent forays, the distant territories west of the Rockies' height of land were left undisturbed by intruders. It was not until 1808, long after Mackenzie's triumphant return to Britain and subsequent knighthood, that another Scot, Simon Fraser, would shoot through the cascades and gorges to the mouth of the torrential river that now bears his name. The North West Company needed to gain trading access to the Pacific to ease the expense of its continental transportation network. Despite his heroic feat, his adventure proved only that the river named after him was not a navigable trade route.

After both Mackenzie and Fraser had proven it was impossible to send freight canoes through the mountains, it became evident that the only effective way to move goods to their Pacific side was to go around them. That required a successful expedition down the serpentine Columbia to its saltwater mouth. The Nor'Wester who accomplished that difficult task (as well as mapping one-third of the previously blank subcontinent) was an enlightened geographer named David Thompson.

Thompson stood out among his colleagues. Welsh instead of Scottish, he was prodigiously literate, leaving behind thirty-nine volumes of journals that rank as major contributions to the early history of Canada. Originally apprenticed to the Hudson's Bay Company, he was frustrated by its limited interest in his surveys and switched to the NWC in 1797. He cared little for the fur trade but walked and canoed fifty-five thousand miles, pacing off the country he was determined to chart. During his stewardship

Here my voyages of discovery terminate. Their toils and their dangers... have not been exaggerated in my description... I received, however, the reward of my labours, for they were crowned with success.

THE FINAL ENTRY IN ALEXANDER
MACKENZIE'S JOURNAL, 1793

At the age of only twenty-nine, Alexander Mackenzie of the North West Company could claim the honour of being the first European to cross North America by land.

(Above) A portrait of Alexander Mackenzie by Sir Thomas Lawrence. Behind him are the spectacular mountains he crossed to reach the Pacific Ocean. (Left) Mackenzie's long-erased message of red pigment and bear grease has been recreated in cement on a rock in Dean Channel near Bella Coola, British Columbia.

David Thompson in the Athabasca Pass, 1810.

as chief topographer of the North West Company, Thompson not only mapped the Columbia River system to the Pacific but also pinpointed the sources of the Mississippi, explored the upper region of the Missouri and the southeastern interior of British Columbia, as well as charting much of the official U.S.-Canada boundary.

Many of Thompson's most important contributions flowed from his efforts to open trade with the Indians west of the Great Divide. However, when Thompson himself finally reached the Pacific via the Columbia River in March 1811, he encountered four newly built log cabins. John Jacob Astor's Pacific Fur Company had beaten the Nor'Westers to the Pacific Coast by sea, and had already established its claims by building the tiny trading post of Astoria.

The Nor'Westers' impulse to explore uncharted territories was less the product of an altruistic desire to advance the frontiers of knowledge than a direct consequence of the company's infrastructure and the stretch of its traplines. The NWC's profitability depended on constantly moving onward and outward to tap newer and richer animal preserves. That in turn meant maintaining an ever-lengthening transportation system with large and multiply-

THE *TONQUIN* MASSACRE

In 1811 the Americans and the Nor'Westers were involved in a race to lay claim to the Pacific Coast. An American ship, the *Tonquin*, representing John Jacob Astor's Pacific Fur Company, won, reaching the West Coast in March 1811, three months before the Nor'westers.

But Astor had unfortunately placed the *Tonquin* under the command of a loony naval officer, James Thorn. Thorn treated his crew members with cruelty and contempt, even threatening to blow off the head of any crew member hesitating to obey his orders.

On June 5, 1811, after establishing a site for Astor's western headquarters, called Astoria, Thorn sailed north to barter with the Indians for sea otter skins. While anchored off Vancouver Island, Thorn lost his temper with a local chief, threw a

pelt in his face and ordered him off the ship. Fearing trouble, Thorn's mates urged him to set sail. The stubborn captain ignored them. The next morning large canoes arrived with their occupants waving otter skins, indicating eagerness to trade, and Thorn beckoned them aboard. As more and more Indians crowded the deck, Thorn was warned that the situation was getting out of control, but he kept exchanging furs for knives. At a pre-arranged signal, the Indians drew knives and attacked with

At the mouth of the Columbia River, Captain Thorn insisted that a boat sound the channel, even though the water was very rough. The boat overturned and five men drowned.

wild whoops, slashing throats and throwing bodies, including Thorn's, overboard. James Lewis, the wounded ship's clerk, managed to pull himself to the *Tonquin*'s magazine. Next morning when the Indians came to claim their loot, he lit a fuse and blew them — and himself — sky-high.

ing overhead expenditures. Unlike the more sedentary Bay men, the Nor'Westers were constantly in motion. Their canoes were propelled by voyageurs, free spirits and galley slaves both, their only reward a defiant pride in their own courage and endurance. Their subculture was based on custom, dress and circumstance, but the French language was their unifying ethos. As the beaver lodges in relatively accessible corners were trapped out, the canoe brigades aimed always farther afield – and the longer the network, the greater the hardships. No wonder the North West Company's official motto eschewed Latin subtleties, encapsulating its hopes in a one-word, no-nonsense exclamation: "PERSEVERANCE!"

The North West Company sought in vain what the Hudson's Bay Company took for granted: direct sea-access into the continent's midriff and a monopoly sanctioned by royal decree over the trading area within its jurisdiction. Yet within two decades of their original unification, the Nor'Westers – under the guidance of Simon McTavish, the company's chief founder and guiding spirit – controlled 78 percent of Canadian fur sales.

If the HBC wasn't ready to launch a full-scale challenge to the North West Company's domination, other Montreal traders were. By 1798 the New North West Company (quickly dubbed the XY Company after the "XY" insignia on its kegs and bales of furs) was ready to do battle. At first, the Nor'Westers dismissed the upstarts, but the newcomers quickly put together a highly efficient woods operation stretching all the way to the Athabasca. The competition remained manageable until former NWC partner Alexander Mackenzie brought his prestige and aggressive management into the concern. Mackenzie had become disillusioned with the NWC after his innovative ideas for expanding the fur trade, including a possible merger with the Hudson's Bay Company, had been rejected. Mackenzie had quit the NWC in 1799 and soon joined the XY Company which changed its name to Alexander Mackenzie & Company. By 1802, the working capital of Mackenzie & Co. nearly equalled that of the older NWC partnership. The competition became a personal battle between the ambitious Mackenzie and the powerful McTavish, but it quickly spread into the wilderness, where angry traders spied on one another, ambushed pemmican-laden canoes and, in one notorious instance, resorted to murder.

Mackenzie had long set his corporate sights on the HBC. As senior partner in his own firm, Mackenzie again went after the Company, attempting to buy a controlling interest. But the effort failed and the escalating vendetta between Mackenzie and the NWC came to an abrupt resolution when Simon McTavish died unexpectedly on July 6, 1804. With McTavish's autocratic presence removed, Mackenzie and William McGillivray, who had succeeded McTavish, took only four months to negotiate a merger of the two competing firms under the North West Company name.

The Nor'Westers had survived a bitter struggle with Mackenzie and his partners only to find themselves scrapping with a revitalized Hudson's Bay Company for the spoils of the west.

Two redoubtable men, Andrew Colvile and John Wedderburn Halkett, had purchased substantial share positions in the HBC during 1809. While Halkett did not become a member of the governing Committee for another two years, Colvile assumed a position of power almost immediately. He was determined that the older Company take on the NWC, but it was a renegade Nor'Wester named Colin Robertson who provided the winning card. The same day Colvile took up his seat on the Committee, Robertson had made a forceful presentation to the board arguing that instead of cowering before the Nor'Westers the HBC should attack them, specifically by mounting an expedition from Montreal to conquer the Athabasca fur lands. "Good God! See the Canadians come thousands of miles beyond us to monopolize the most valuable part of your Territories," he admonished the Committee. He also advo-

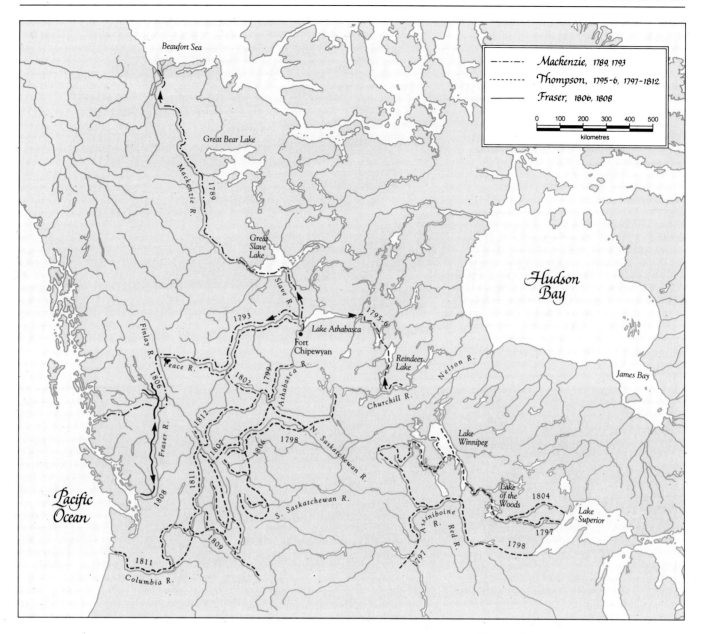

The exploration routes of Mackenzie, Thompson and Fraser.

cated that the Company revise its compensation arrangements so that its senior traders would, much like the Nor'Westers, be paid as incentive-inspired partners. With Colvile's support for the new arrangements, Robertson won the day.

Robertson, who had served the NWC as a clerk and had been fired the previous year after a fistfight, was a new kind of man in the service of the Hudson's Bay Company. His personal motto, "When you are among wolves, howl," summed up his operating philosophy. The Committeemen expeditiously adopted the proud Highlander's recommendations that the Company seek its future traders in Scotland's Western Isles, in the Shetlands and among the heather of the Highlands.

But the most essential recruit in the unexpected surge of new-found energy was Andrew Colvile's brother-in-law, a Scottish nobleman known as Thomas Douglas, 5th Earl of Selkirk.

CANOES OF THE FUR TRADE

Made of birchbark and cedar and held together with tree roots and tar, the canoes used by the French pedlars and their HBC rivals ranged in size from forty-foot freighters to swift, small vessels used to carry VIPs from post to post.

(Right) HBC canoes. The bottom two were called "five fathom" canoes.
(Below) A freight canoe today at Old Fort William and (inset) at the Red River Colony in the 1820s.
(Opposite) An expert at Old Fort William caulks a birchbark canoe.
(Overleaf) Shooting the Rapids by Frances Hopkins.

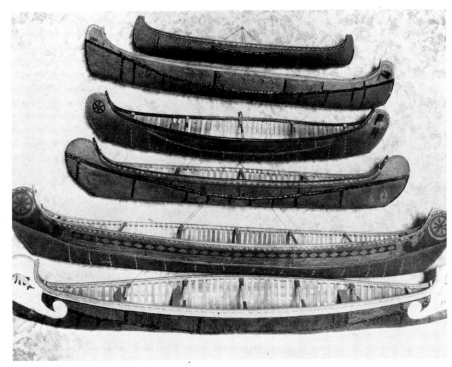

THE HARDY VOYAGEURS

The voyageurs were the rock upon which the North West Company built its empire. Because of their willingness to paddle from sunrise to sunset or heave back-breaking packs over arduous portages, the North West Company gave the HBC a run for its money and came close to defeating the gentleman adventurers in the early years of the nineteenth century.

Unsung, unlettered and uncouth, the voyageurs lived in a universe defined by the canoe and the French language. Rarely, if ever, promoted to join the North West Company's bourgeois, they made a virtue of their servile status, developing their own dress, customs and legends that no outsider could ever hope to share.

To be a voyageur was to be in motion for much of the year. Each spring the canoe brigades would gather at Lachine, just outside Montreal, and prepare for the trip west carrying the trade goods needed for the fur trade. The voyageurs' goal was to be at the North West Company's inland headquarters, originally at Grand Portage and later moved to Fort William, within eight weeks.

To do this, they had to maintain a killing pace. Each morning they would rise at four or earlier and set out, maintaining a rhythm of forty-five paddle strokes a minute, which could drive a canoe at about six knots. Every hour they rested, usually long enough to smoke a single pipe of tobacco. To pass the time and keep the rhythm, the voyageurs sang as they paddled. Their unofficial anthem was "A la claire fontaine," a tale of lost love. As darkness fell, the canoes were pulled ashore and the day's damage repaired, a difficult job by firelight. The voyageurs then settled in for a meal of pemmican or dried peas or cornmeal mixed with water and some lard or suet stirred in. Shelter for the night was the overturned canoe. Too soon,

(Opposite) For portaging, each voyageur carried, as standard, two ninety-pound packs. One was suspended on a tumpline that ran across the forehead; the second pack was placed atop the first and sat between the shoulder blades.

(Right) A drawing of three voyageurs in the 1820s, showing the preferred garb of these hardy men: moccasins, a capot, or hooded frock coat, and a tall hat. A sash, the famous ceintures flechées, *was another voyageur trademark.*

(Below) A freight canoe with two passengers. The voyageurs maintained their own hierarchy. At the bottom were the milieux, *the paddlers who sat two abreast. The* avant *(bowsman) and the* gouvernail *(steersman) were more senior voyageurs, whose muscle, experience and intuitive feel for the rivers and lakes won them these important posts.*

the sun would be starting to appear through the trees.

To paddle, day in day out, required stamina enough, but it was on the portages that men were truly put to the test. The first leg of the route from Montreal, up the Ottawa River and across to Georgian Bay, required thirty-six portages, ranging from a few hun- dred yards to several miles. The standard load per man was 180 pounds — two ninety-pound bags of goods. But voyageurs could earn a Spanish silver dollar by carrying more, and there are stories of men carrying up to five hundred pounds. Not surprisingly, most voyageurs preferred to avoid portaging, choosing instead to run rapids if at all possible.

The spring brigades arrived at Fort William in July. Most of the men in the freight canoes then loaded up with furs and headed back to Montreal. But some, those who planned to spend their three-year enlistment in the north country, stayed behind. They joined the crews of five man *canots du*

nord, making their way into the Fur Country. Again, time was short — they had to be at their winter homes before the rivers froze. Pushing off inland, they worked west to Lake Winnipeg, and from there fanned out across the Fur Country to as far away as Great Slave Lake.

To winter in the hinterland was to be part of the true elite. Any voyageur entering the north country for the first time was "baptised" in an informal ceremony after which he could proudly claim, "*Je suis un homme du nord.*" For those voyageurs, though, winter was a boring affair, consisting mainly of gathering firewood and running goods and messages from fort to fort by dogsled. Only with spring break-up, and the prospect of a dash to Fort William in a fur-laden canoe, did their lives take on meaning once again.

_____

(Above) Voyageurs at Dawn, *painted by Frances Hopkins, shows a typical voyageurs' campsite. The overturned canoe served as shelter at night.*

CHAPTER SEVEN

SHOOTOUT AT SEVEN OAKS

W HETHER HE WAS FOOL OR SAINT IS THE TROUBLING uncertainty that still clouds the considerable Selkirk legacy. This frail Scottish earl, with a burning mission matched by the fire consuming his tubercular lungs, established western Canada's founding community with the Highland settlers he brought to the Red River. His unusual venture effectively triggered the North West Company's demise.

Selkirk was driven by a personal sense of guilt over the suffering of the Scottish crofters during the Highland Clearances and by frustration at his incurable tuberculosis. Even while he was devoting himself wholly to the Red River Colony, his lace handkerchiefs could not disguise the blood coughed up from his chest. However noble Selkirk's aspirations may have been, they were to clash resoundingly with the harsh realities of the fur trade and nature's destructive cycles.

Selkirk was born on June 20, 1771, at St. Mary's Isle, his family's ancient seat in southwestern Scotland. Unlike his elder brothers, Thomas Douglas was not trained for the law or military service but rather was a product of the new enlightenment sweeping continental Europe during his university years. From a visit to revolutionary France the young Douglas derived two motivating impulses: that thoughtful aristocrats were not precluded from implementing social reform, and that not to initiate reform was by far the riskier course.

After his return to Scotland, he astonished his father and brothers by choosing to work on the family farm, labouring from dawn to dusk as hard as any tenant, ploughing the black earth, scything the stalks of oats and barley. As part of his growing enthusiasm for improved land use, Selkirk began to take private journeys northward into the Highlands, where he came face to face with the notorious Clearances.

During the century after the defeat of the clans at Culloden, a windswept moor where the Jacobites under Bonnie Prince Char-

(Opposite) This pastoral Red River scene was closer to Lord Selkirk's utopian dream than to the harsh reality of life in his colony.

lie were slaughtered by English redcoats on April 16, 1746, the decision by the Scottish nobles to turn their glens and braes into huge sheep farms meant driving out the families who had farmed the land for generations. No one then (or now) could calculate exactly how many men, women and children were dispossessed in favour of sheep. According to one estimate, two-thirds of the Highlanders in the northern counties of Inverness, Caithness and Sutherland lost their homes.

These scenes of suffering witnessed by the impressionable young Selkirk created his obsession to find homes for the displaced crofters. His prestige and ability to influence events were unexpectedly enhanced in 1799, when at his father's death, as the sole survivor among his brothers, he became the 5th Earl of Selkirk. The new lord used his inherited fortune and authority to purchase landholdings on Prince Edward Island, where in 1803 he successfully settled eight hundred Highlanders. The following year he tried a similar but much less successful experiment at Baldoon in Upper Canada.

Thomas Douglas, 5th Earl of Selkirk

These preliminary forays brought Selkirk to Montreal, where he was treated to a lavish dinner by the nabobs of the North West Company and heard for the first time intriguing tales about North America's lucrative interior. He had read Alexander Mackenzie's recently published *Voyages* and was enthralled by its references to fertile lands owned by the HBC in the Red River Valley, with its 170-day growing season and plentiful buffalo herds to supply fresh meat. When Mackenzie approached Selkirk with the idea of trying to gain control of the Hudson's Bay Company, the Earl readily agreed, though their unspoken aims were diametrically opposed. Mackenzie was the stalking horse for the Nor'Westers, while for Selkirk, the fur trade seemed to provide an ideal entry-point for his colonization scheme at Red River.

The Earl was already interested in the HBC. In 1807, the year before Mackenzie approached him, he had married Jean Wedderburn. The family of the vivacious twenty-one-year-old beauty was about to make large investments in the Company, so her brother Andrew was named to the HBC's governing committee. Selkirk had not long before obtained written opinions from London's leading legal firms indicating that Prince Rupert's original Charter was not only valid but that it clearly assigned the right to grant parts of the Company's huge domain for the establishment of a permanent colony at Red River. By May 24, 1809, Selkirk had invested £4,087 in HBC stock, Andrew Colvile had purchased a further £4,454 and their kinsman John Halkett, £3,717.

As soon as Mackenzie realized Selkirk's true aims, he threatened a lawsuit but dropped it in favour of urging NWC partners William and Simon McGillivray to start buying stock of their own to thwart the Scottish peer's plans. They didn't move fast enough. Selkirk eventually purchased enough shares that along with his relatives' previous holdings he could dominate the HBC's affairs.

But the Committeemen were hesitant to invest funds of the cash-poor Company in such a risky venture, insisting that Selkirk finance the new settlement himself. With the risks removed, the HBC allowed itself to recognize the venture's advantages, the main one being that it would affirm once and for all the validity of its Charter, in the sense that granting the land for colonization would confirm that the HBC had owned it in the first place. After considering Selkirk's request for nearly a year, the HBC Committee agreed to the terms of the land grant and, in return for a nominal payment of ten shillings, Selkirk was granted a land empire of stunning proportions. Stretching over 116,000 square miles (the equivalent of 74,240,000 acres), the area covered territory four times the size of Scotland. The grant's borders extended into the present-day states of Minnesota, North Dakota and the northeast corner of South Dakota. Its western margin was deep in what is now Saskatchewan, almost to the source of the Assiniboine River. That bountiful domain contained what would later prove to be some of the earth's most fertile agricultural land. It was as magnificent a gift as was ever bestowed on a would-be colonizer.

Furious, Nor'Westers toured London's coffee houses, whipping up opposition to the grant. Their objections were easy enough to understand. At the most rudimentary level, the HBC had just handed over to Selkirk the land on which half a dozen of the Montreal company's most important trading forts were located (Pembina, Bas-de-la-Rivière, Dauphin, Gibraltar, Espérance and La Souris) and across which lay its main supply routes from Fort William westward. More important, the valleys of the Red River basin were the main source of buffalo-based pemmican, the food staple the NWC needed to fuel its voyageur brigades. It seemed obvious to the Nor'Westers that the Bay men wanted to use Red River as a natural supply base to wedge themselves into the Athabasca Country, the NWC's most lucrative fur preserve. Their howls of protest didn't help. Selkirk got his grant.

The ordeal endured by the Selkirk colonists during their first decade at Red River is usually tallied in terms of various armed confrontations with the Montrealers' local agents, but, initially, the Nor'Westers did nothing to hamper the settlers. They didn't have to. Nature was a much more dependable enemy.

The settlers had been recruited throughout Scotland and a former captain in the Loyalist Royal Canadian Volunteers, Miles Macdonell, was hired to prepare the colony for permanent settlement. Although they may have been simple Highland crofters, the newcomers were men and women of inordinate fortitude and resourcefulness. They came not with ploughs but with hoes and spades to scratch the impervious surface of the great prairie; they boiled buffalo grease for soap and made starch from potatoes; they learned to pound pemmican and flavour it with sturgeon eggs. They survived, mainly because there was nowhere else for them to go.

When Sioux or Mixed Bloods attacked, the settlers hid their children under mats of sod or marsh grass; they knew that the nearest possible source for significant reinforcements was York Factory, more than seven hundred miles away. It might as well have been seven thousand. Wolves, wild dogs and blizzards killed their few precious cattle; for two successive summers, clattering plagues of grasshoppers destroyed everything edible, plugging even the wells and chimneys. The Red River washed away what fragile crops had been planted on its flood plains, while drought withered the remainder of the valiantly rooted vegetation. When the colonists survived the growing seasons (harvesting only two good crops in the first ten years), they were left to face the bitter frosts of winter.

About two hundred and seventy settlers arrived in the first five years, beating upstream from York Factory, sometimes led by a piper, always propelled by hope. The colony's relationship with the Indians (except for occasional raids by the Sioux) was amicable. Not so the Métis. The original settlers of these river banks, they quickly became the most distinctive element in the battles for tenure and supremacy that followed the arrival of the Scottish (and a few Irish) crofters. "Métis," a word probably based on the Spanish "mestizo" (mixture), is an elusive term applying to anyone whose culture and genealogy combine the customs, living styles and values of their roots, European and aboriginal.

The land on which they had settled gave the Métis a powerful sense of belonging – and that, in turn, meant that, unlike the other non-Indian inhabitants of the Fur Country, this defiant people had a specific territory of their own to defend. They were not, at least not yet, a "New Nation," as some of their more radical adherents maintained, but they were already a political force – Western Canada's first nationalists, a populist movement in search of a cause.

That cause was provided by the arrival of the Selkirk settlers. Here was a group of cast-offs from another continent insisting they

THE FUEL OF
THE FUR TRADE

The canoe brigades that pushed their way across the Northwest had no time to hunt for food along the way. Nor had they space to bring their food with them from the East, from Montreal or Fort William. Instead, they depended upon pemmican, which they picked up in the north country.

Pemmican (the term is derived from the Cree word for "he makes grease") was dried buffalo meat prepared according to a very simple recipe: Take one buffalo, and first putting the hide aside, cut into flakes or thin strips. Then hang out on racks to dry in the sun, or over a fire. Once the meat is dried, take down and pound until reduced to a pulp. At this stage, take the buffalo hide, after sewing it into a large rawhide sack, and fill half full with pulverized meat. Add boiling buffalo fat and sixteen pounds of saskatoon berries (useful for averting the scurvy that an all-pemmican diet might

Buffalo meat being dried on racks, the first stage in making pemmican.

otherwise cause). Finally sew up the bag and seal with tallow.

The average voyageur received a ration of a pound and a half of pemmican a day, which he either ate raw, made into a soup called rababoo or sliced up, covered with flour and fried. One of the advantages of pemmican, especially on long-haul canoe trips, was that it never seemed to go bad. Indeed, there is a recorded instance of someone eating, without any reported ill effects, pemmican made some fifty years before.

Pemmican fanciers claimed that it tasted like nothing else, that the only thing pemmican resembled was pemmican. Perhaps the most accurate description of its flavour comes down to us today in H.M. Robinson's *The Great Fur Land*: "Take the scrapings from the driest outside corner of a very stale piece of cold roast beef, add to it lumps of rancid fat, then garnish all with long human hairs and short hairs of dogs and oxen and you have a fair imitation of common pemmican."

had been granted title to the very land the Métis claimed by right of occupation, not to mention descent from Cree and Saulteaux ancestors who had been its original inhabitants.

Given the rallying cry of driving out the unwelcome intruders and the fact that the discipline of the buffalo hunts and their brushes with the Sioux had toughened the Métis into effective warriors, all they needed to launch Canada's first war of liberation was someone to command them.

The leader who emerged to fill this pivotal role at the crucial moment was Cuthbert Grant, Métis patriot and loyal Nor'Wester. But it was the provocative tactics of Miles Macdonell, governor of the putative Selkirk Settlement, that united the Métis as never before. A Roman Catholic of Loyalist stock with the sublime faith that characterizes both, Macdonell had with one stroke removed any vestiges of doubt as to whether the settlers would interfere with the essential flow of pemmican from Red River to depots along the NWC trading routes. Arguing that the life-sustaining food needed for his own hungry settlers was being produced on land owned by Lord Selkirk, he issued the proclamations that would become the opening shots in the Pemmican War: an edict forbidding further exports of the staple from Red River without his permission, and a prohibition against the hunting of buffalo from horseback within the Selkirk territories. He followed these foolhardy initiatives by confiscating four hundred bags of NWC pemmican and moving it under armed guard to the colony's headquarters, Fort Douglas, boasting that he had force enough "to crush all the Nor'Westers...should they be so hardy as to resist...authority."

As if bent on self-destruction, Macdonell then sent notices to the commanders of NWC forts on the Selkirk lands ordering them to evacuate their posts within six months. That was too much. At their annual council meeting in the Great Hall at Fort William, the Nor'Westers pledged to force the colony out of existence, first by weakening it with efforts to persuade the newcomers to desert, and later by inciting the Indians and Métis against any settlers who remained. As a third step, Miles Macdonell was to be arrested on charges of illegal seizure of pemmican and sent to Montreal for trial, leaving the survivors leaderless. The partner placed in charge of these tactics was Duncan Cameron, a veteran harasser of the HBC. With the aid of Grant, now clearly in charge of his people, the strategy worked. By summer's end of 1815, all but thirteen families had abandoned Red River. Hoping to avert bloodshed, Macdonell surrendered to Cameron at the NWC fort and was promptly spirited away, first to Fort William and then to Montreal.

Robert Semple

Disoriented and unprotected, the remaining straggle of settlers retreated by boat to temporary quarters near the north end of Lake Winnipeg. In the former colony, bands of Métis razed farms, burned buildings, attacked Fort Douglas and the adjoining grist mill. The settlers' last sight of their utopia was smoke wafting in the soft summer breeze and the rampaging Métis spurring their buffalo-runners across the fields, trampling the precious crops. Later, as if signalling some symbolic resurrection, the wheat, barley and potatoes did recover and ripen, unwatched, under the golden summer sun.

On his way from Montreal to reopen the Athabasca Country trade, the HBC's Colin Robertson had by chance met the Red River refugees and persuaded them to return just in time to harvest their somewhat trampled crops. That autumn another group of Scottish immigrants arrived, led by Robert Semple, the colony's new governor. Semple was a Boston-born Loyalist and popular travel writer whose innocence of cunning was matched by his overburden of self-importance. His commission provided dramatic proof of the Nor'Westers' and Métis' contention that the Selkirk Settlement was little more than an agency of the HBC, since he had been simultaneously appointed the colony's new governor and chief of the Company's Northern and Southern departments. Robertson took it upon himself to woo the Métis. He met with such success that when, on March 17, 1816, Robertson attacked and temporarily captured Gibraltar, the NWC stronghold, and arrested Duncan Cameron, none of the Métis joined in the fort's defence. Inside Cameron's desk Robertson found documentary evidence that the Nor'Westers intended to engineer the final destruction of Selkirk's settlement that summer.

Robertson left the colony early in June, warning Semple to prepare for war. On the very day of his departure, the impulsive Semple made a fatal mistake – he ordered that the captured Fort Gibraltar be demolished. "The sight of the great fort in flames was too much" for the Métis, wrote Marjorie Wilkins Campbell, the unofficial historian of the North West Company, for "soon the fire which had been smouldering in every one of them also burst into flame. To each the destruction of the North West Company post was a warning of what might happen to his own small home...."

It was the final, unforgivable act. Led by Cuthbert Grant, recently promoted by the NWC to be their "Captain-General," the Métis struck first at the HBC installation at Brandon House. After plundering the fort, Grant moved against Red River. Inside Fort Douglas, Governor Semple waved off warnings of danger. Still convinced that diplomacy might win the day, Semple decided to meet the marauders and read them a stern proclamation forbidding Métis to commit acts of violence against the colony. The governor rounded up two dozen men to accompany him.

Colin Robertson

Grant and his mounted platoon reached a cluster of trees known locally as Seven Oaks. The two groups met there in the early twilight of a late spring day. Grant signalled one of his subalterns, a Métis named François Firmin Boucher, to order the governor and his men to lay down their arms or be shot. As Boucher urged his horse forward, Grant covered Semple with his gun. The stilted dialogue that followed caught the supercharged tensions of the moment:

"What do you want?" asked Boucher.

"What do you want?" demanded the affronted governor.

"We want our fort," was the spitted reply.

"Well, go to your fort!" Semple snapped back.

"Why have you destroyed our fort? You damned rascal!"

No Métis was going to call him, the Governor of Rupert's Land, a rascal. Semple shouted something like, "Scoundrel? Do you tell me so?" and made a grab for the stock of Boucher's gun while seizing the reins of his horse.

Cuthbert Grant pulled the trigger, wounding Semple in the thigh, and that set off the slaughter. Within fifteen minutes, Semple had been killed by a Métis named François Deschamps, who placed his gun against the governor's chest and pulled the trigger. Twenty of Semple's men lay dead at Seven Oaks. Only one Métis had been killed. Grant took a single prisoner, sending him to deliver a surrender demand to Fort Douglas. The settlement gave in without resistance, terminating Selkirk's colony for the second time in two years. The day's horror was not yet done. At Seven Oaks, the bodies of the dead were stripped and dismembered in an orgy of mutilation.

Seven Oaks changed everything. No longer a commercial contest with the occasional skirmish and post-burning, the struggle between the Nor'Westers and Bay men had turned into a guerrilla war, fought along a four-thousand-mile front. For the first time in the long rivalry between the two companies, the fur trade itself had become subordinate to their struggle for supremacy. No restraint or discipline was applied to the trapping of beaver (even their sucklings were being skinned), to the distribution of rum and brandy or to the tactics used in pillaging competitors' forts. At one point forty-two murder charges had been sworn out against Nor'Westers.

Into this maelstrom stepped Selkirk himself. The news of the Seven Oaks killings reached the nobleman en route to visit Red River at the head of his own private army. When Selkirk heard the facts, he abruptly led his mercenary band against the very heart of the villainous Montrealers' enterprise by capturing their great depot at Fort William and arresting the fifteen senior Montreal partners in residence. William McGillivray, who was among them, was charged with treason, conspiracy and being an accessory to murder. After a desultory attempt to interrogate the Nor'Westers, Selkirk sent them back to Montreal under guard.

Realizing that his ravaged colony at Red River could not hope to feed his accompanying army, Selkirk decided to winter at Fort William. He dispatched his mercenaries westward to retake Fort Douglas. The victorious troops then captured several other NWC outposts, notifying the settlers who had again scattered north to Lake Winnipeg that they could return. By June they were joined by Lord Selkirk. Here at last, more than half a decade after he had first dreamed of providing a sanctuary for his beleaguered crofters, Selkirk was able to see for himself the hardship they had faced and the small promise their situation held out to them. Seized by the feverish exhilaration caused by advancing tuberculosis and

The Seven Oaks massacre, as drawn by C.W. Jefferys.

the rapturous beauty of the prairie summer, he walked among his people like a kilted messiah, granting freedom from further land payments to some two dozen of his most deserving disciples.

By early autumn, knowing that he must deal with the barrage of charges and countercharges stemming from his illegal occupation of Fort William, Lord Selkirk returned eastward to face the uneven scales of Canadian justice. The legal battle dragged on, year after year, exhausting Selkirk physically and financially.

Selkirk's exploits had demonstrated the vulnerability of the Montreal traders and instilled in the HBC officers and servants renewed vitality and pride of place. They felt ready at last to challenge their rivals on their home territory. During the five years after Seven Oaks, the continent-wide rivalry between the NWC and HBC was nowhere contested more bitterly than within

THE NOR'WESTERS AT FORT WILLIAM

Though headquartered in Montreal, the real home of the North West Company was Fort William on Lake Superior. Each summer the Fort became a wilderness city. The canoe brigades would rendezvous here, bringing trade goods from the east and furs from the north country. The wintering partners and their Montreal counterparts also showed up, to negotiate the next season's contract.

Named for North West Company partner William McGillivray, Fort William covered 125 acres and contained about forty-two buildings. At its centre was the Great Hall, where the Montreal partners stayed during their annual visits. Fronted with a balcony sixty feet long, the Great Hall was big enough to seat two hundred at a formal banquet.

The highlight of the summer season at Fort William was a ball to which various "ladies of the country" were invited. Bagpipes droned and violins scraped away long into the night, turning out a mixture of Highland reels and Habitant jigs.

After the ball, Fort William wound down quickly. The wintering partners headed back into the Fur Country, the Montreal partners returned east, with freight canoes laden down with furs. By late August, there were fewer than two dozen caretakers left at the post.

(Above, right) Dr John McLoughlin, one of the NWC's most respected wintering partners, later went on to a successful career with the HBC. (Right) A sketch of Fort William as it would have looked at its height in the early 1800s. The Great Hall is the middle of the three buildings facing the main square.

(Above) The crest of the North West Company.

(Left) Dr John McLoughlin presiding over festivities similar to those at Fort William. Scots predominated among the clerks and partners of the North West Company; any proprietor with pretensions built himself a Montreal mansion in Scottish baronial style.

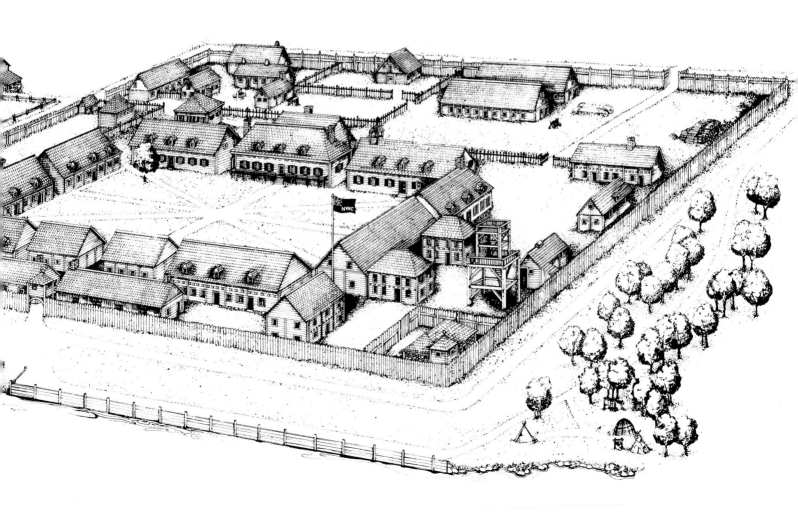

A sketch made by Lord Selkirk during his illegal occupation of Fort William. The front gates of the fort can be seen through the window.

Athabasca Country. Here the last violent clashes between the two companies determined the outcome of their protracted quarrel.

Infuriated by Selkirk's capture of Fort William, the Nor'Westers immediately seized the five tiny posts the Bay men had established in Athabasca during their tentative 1815 foray. By the summer of 1818, the HBC's Athabasca venture had managed to retain merely a tiny fishing camp in the area.

Realizing that only a massive assault could turn the tide, the Company commissioned Colin Robertson to lead an attack brigade of nearly two hundred armed men into the disputed territory. His determination proved effective in attracting the Indians; within weeks of his arrival, Robertson had restored the Company's Fort Wedderburn and was trading with four dozen Indian chiefs who had previously been loyal NWC customers. The Montrealers called in reinforcements led by Simon McGillivray, Jr., the Mixed Blood son of that company's reigning grandee. But the day-to-day harassment was left to Samuel Black, a malevolent bully who took a special delight in threatening and attacking Bay men.

On October 11, 1818, Robertson was seized at gunpoint by Black and McGillivray and bundled off to the NWC's Fort Chipewyan. Robertson was soon pinioned and confined inside a small shack next to the fort's privy. There he stayed for eight months. Worried that his troops had been left leaderless, Robertson devised an ingenious method for sending out coded messages. Eventually he was spotted scribbling out his cryptic instructions and the Nor'Westers decided to pack him off to Montreal. He escaped when they were passing Cumberland House by the simple stratagem of asking, on his word of honour, if he could step inside the HBC fort to say his farewells. Once inside, Robertson had the doors bolted and refused to come out. The angry Nor'Westers continued on without him.

Robertson obtained revenge for his imprisonment. In one of the messages he had managed to sneak past his guards, Robertson had warned William Williams, the HBC's recently appointed Governor of Rupert's Land, that the Nor'West partners would probably be returning to Montreal loaded with furs and could be ambushed at Grand Rapids, the rendezvous near the juncture of the Saskatchewan River and Lake Winnipeg. A truculent former East India Company sea captain, Williams acted on the dispatch. The HBC trap netted not only loads of fur but five disgruntled senior NWC partners. The Grand Rapids affair seriously undermined the Montrealers' morale. "Our opponents," Robertson wrote to Williams, "have lowered their tone; they talk now of conducting their business on amicable principles...." But the fur war raged on.

Robertson's idol, Lord Selkirk, meanwhile, was struggling to extricate himself from the final and most traumatic episode of his Canadian misadventures. He had spent most of the interval since returning from that brief happy summer at Red River in stultifying courtrooms, first in Montreal and later in York (Toronto), pursuing the 170 charges he had proferred against the NWC and its partners. "If we are to be poor for three generations, we must absolutely fight this out," a faithful Lady Selkirk wrote her husband. The Earl spent the last of his energies and much of his fortune in the futile exercise involving a variety of contemptuous witnesses and corrupt judges. At the end of the lengthy litigation, Selkirk was himself assessed £2,000 for damages while not a single Nor'Wester was fined or imprisoned. Not waiting to hear this ludicrous verdict announced, Selkirk returned to London, his health finally broken.

Selkirk's illness forced him to seek the drier climate of southwestern France, where he died on the morning of April 8, 1820, aged forty-nine. It had been Lord Selkirk's fate to juggle desirable ends with destructive means. In the end he lost everything except his self-esteem.

Governor William Williams

THE SELKIRK SETTLERS

After the defeat of Bonnie Prince Charlie and his Highland supporters at Culloden in 1746, the British moved to break the power of the Scottish clans. Under strict measures that even forbade the playing of the bagpipes, the paternalistic bond between the Highland chieftain and his people began to crumble. The next generation of Highland "lairds" took on southern wives and manners and preferred the town-houses of London or Edinburgh to the stone walls of their Highland castles. This style

of living required enhanced incomes that could only be brought about by "improvement" of their ancestral lands. Throughout most of the nineteenth century, "improvement" meant turning their estates into huge sheep farms.

But clearing the glens for pasturage meant that the crofter tenants, who for centuries had farmed them and served in battle for the laird's forebears, had to be removed. With bayonet and truncheon the Highlanders were driven from their homes and forced to emigrate or eke out a miserable existence in tiny coastal villages.

On a single day in the valley of Strathnaver in northern Scotland,

for example, sixteen hundred people were told that they had an hour to gather up their belongings before their homes would be set on fire. As one observer wrote, "The terrible remembrance of the burnings of Strathnaver will live as long as the root of the people remains in the country...."

A new life in a new land was the promise that Lord Selkirk's Red River Colony held for displaced Highlanders. The first group of just over one hundred crofters left Scotland on July 26, 1811, under the command of Miles Macdonell, an overbearing military man hired by Selkirk to lead this advance party. After a nightmare voyage of

sixty-one days in a filthy, cramped vessel, the settlers arrived at York Factory too late in the season to chance an overland voyage to

(Opposite, top) A Highland tenant family looks back at their burning home following an evacuation forced by the laird's marshals.
(Opposite, bottom) The Last of the Clan by Victorian painter Thomas Faed presents a romantic tableau of the sad scenes that accompanied the departure of immigrant ships from Scotland.
(Below) Before the Highland Clearances stone crofts like this one in the Orkneys dotted the landscape of the Scottish Isles and Highlands.

Red River. The long winter was spent in a makeshift camp with limited provisions, which caused an outbreak of scurvy, and by spring fewer than half of the group were mobile. Four crude boats bearing only twenty-two men set off down the Hayes River on July 6, 1812. After journeying south through wild, unknown country and across Lake Winnipeg, the first settlers arrived at the junction of the Assiniboine and Red rivers.

Macdonnell chose the west bank of the Red River as the site of Fort Douglas, which he hoped would be the new colony's headquarters. Guests from nearby posts of both the Hudson's Bay and North West companies were invited to the formal ceremonies on September 4 at which Macdonnell took possession of the land on behalf of Lord Selkirk and had himself sworn in as governor. For the bewildered and exhausted Highlanders, this day must have been filled with promise. But the ordeal of the Selkirk settlers was only just beginning.

(Below) Boats leaving York Factory for Red River in 1821 as painted by Peter Rindisbacher, the teenaged son of Swiss immigrants to the colony. Rindisbacher's paintings and sketches, two of which are shown opposite, are the earliest pictorial record of life in Canada west of the Great Lakes. The hardships of life in Red River finally drove the Rindisbacher family to the United States, where Peter died at the age of twenty-eight.

(Bottom) Two-wheeled Red River carts drawn either by horse or oxen, provided transport for settlers and their goods. Made entirely of wood with no oiled or metal parts, their movements were accompanied by a loud shrieking noise. The wheels, which had tires made of buffalo hide, could be removed and the cart paddled across lakes and rivers.

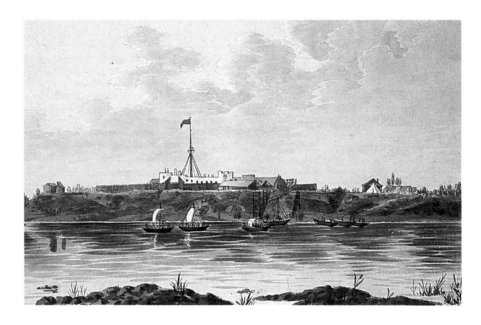

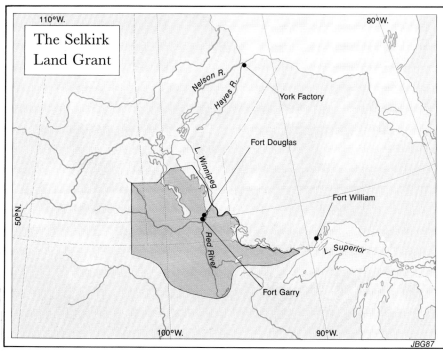

The Selkirk
Land Grant

(Left) The size of the Selkirk land
grant was only about 5,999 square
miles smaller than the combined land
surfaces of the British Isles.
(Top) An 1822 watercolour by Peter
Rindisbacher of the Red River with
Fort Douglas in the background.
(Above) A Rindisbacher sketch of the
types of Lord Selkirk's settlers in 1822
which included a Swiss family from
Berne, a former German soldier, a
Scottish Highlander and a Habitant.

CHAPTER EIGHT

A DEFIANT ALLIANCE

"AS THE COMPETITION FOR THE FUR TRADE PROCEEDED to climax, the Hudson's Bay Company threw some of its traditions overboard," historian K.G. Davies observed, "and fought the Nor'Westers with their own weapons." By 1820, the once-quiescent style of the royally chartered Company had been abandoned for the freewheeling capitalism of the rival Montrealers; in the heat of bitter struggle, the HBC transformed itself into a mirror image of the enterprise it was aiming to defeat.

Although it lost most of the battles, the HBC eventually won the war, largely by appropriating its enemies' tactics. When they awoke to the fact that their territories were threatened by the Nor'westers, the London Governors responded by expanding the Company's inland facilities and incurring expenses with a momentum more typical of their opponents. In competing fur areas, they set their barter rates with the Indians at ruinously low levels in an aggressive move to drive out competition.

Conversely, the North West Company was ultimately defeated because it did not, in fact could not, respond by emulating its enemy. While the HBC was busily adopting Nor'Wester methods and ethics it never lost the sustaining advantages of long-term credit from the Bank of England, a bulwark of powerful politicians willing to respect its royally bestowed monopoly, and a management committee whose members could afford to skip dividends and, if necessary, tide the Company over with personal loans. These were substantial privileges more easily envied than copied.

Even at the height of its power with a domain that spanned a continent, the North West Company lacked secure long-term financing from London's investment houses. Its managers were also its proprietors, dependent on dividend income to support their extravagant way of life. Year after year, ever-larger payouts had to be made – even though they drained most of the NWC's working capital at each season's end. Maintaining this cash flow required that profits be multiplied annually, which in turn demanded

(Opposite) A Regency view of Fenchurch Street, where the Hudson's Bay Company was headquartered.

constant territorial expansion. Yet the farther west or north the NWC pushed, the greater was the strain on its already pathetically overextended transportation network – the interminable and expensive hauls thousands of miles into the heart of the continent and then back to Montreal. And once the Nor'Westers' westward march was halted by the Pacific Ocean and the Bay men began to respond with their own brand of vigour and trading panache, the Montreal company faltered. And having faltered, it cracked.

By the autumn of 1820, the companies had reached an impasse that only a merger could resolve. Beyond their commercial imperatives was the pressure being applied by the Colonial Office for an extension of British influence across the North American continent, an objective that could be achieved only by a single, financially sound trading company. That was why, not long after Selkirk's death in April of that year, Lord Bathurst assured representatives of both firms that if they could hammer out the financial details, he would sponsor an Act of Parliament approving their amalgamation. And there was an enticing inducement to the union promised by the Colonial Secretary: the new, amalgamated company would be granted exclusive trading privileges west of Rupert's Land all the way to the Pacific Coast. To promote such a merger, Bathurst enlisted one of Britain's most successful power brokers, the enigmatic Edward "Bear" Ellice.

Edward "Bear" Ellice

With his cherry-cheerful red face and playful manner, Ellice had earned his nickname not from any predisposition to ferocity, but because, like a bear, he was considered well greased in his dealings with friend and foe alike. Although he was a pivotal influence within the governing Whig party for half a century, Ellice's main function was to act as an honest or at least expedient broker between men, ideas and money on both sides of the Atlantic. Not much happened within Britain's governing circles without "the Bear's" unofficial blessing.

Possessing a solid family background and an inherited fortune, Ellice used two marriages to women of rank to advance his social standing. Elected Whig member of Parliament for Coventry in 1818, he served as an MP for all but four of the next forty-five years, rising to Secretary of the Treasury and, later, Secretary of War. Almost as if he led a double life, the Bear was also deeply involved in the Canadian fur trade, spending long periods of time in Montreal, in his role as senior NWC partner as well as the company's chief London agent. Five months before Selkirk's death, Ellice had approached the HBC's Andrew Colvile with an offer to buy the consumptive earl's shares at his own valuation, while pledging to maintain existing obligations to the Red River settlers.

Selkirk dismissed this option as "all bunkum," but it wasn't. What was left unmentioned in this flash exchange (although Ellice and Colvile may not have been aware of it) was that the North West Company's bargaining status had been grievously undermined at its 1820 conclave in Fort William, and that it would soon either have to buy out the HBC or be bought out instead.

At that meeting the Nor'Westers were asked to renew for another decade the partnership agreements signed in 1802 and 1804, due to expire on November 30, 1822. Aware that their company was in perilous financial condition, worried about their own futures and those of their wilderness families, weary to the bone of the violence and hardships of the war with the HBC, they took out their resentment on their own Montreal agents. William McGillivray tried to hold the mutineers in check, but for the first time in the NWC's reign the country partners would not listen. Instead, eighteen of the most senior "winterers," so called because they wintered in the Fur Country, voted their proxies to two of their own, Dr John McLoughlin and Angus Bethune, charging them with a momentous mission: to sign a peace treaty with the Hudson's Bay Company. It was this rebellion of the wintering partners more than any other catalyst that swung the ensuing negotiations in favour of the HBC.

Simon McGillivray

Bent on their covert mission to London on behalf of the winterers, McLoughlin and Bethune first stopped in Montreal, where they contacted Samuel Gale, Selkirk's legal counsel, to inquire whether the HBC might enter into a new partnership with them. Gale expeditiously communicated the offer to London, so that Andrew Colvile was aware of the Nor'Westers' internal dissension before serious and more public negotiations on amalgamation got under way. The arrival in London of the two hot-eyed winterers accelerated everyone's timetable. Ellice and the McGillivrays knew this was the last available moment if they wanted the HBC to negotiate with them instead of the mutineers' envoys. Colvile, who had been charged with formulating the union on behalf of the HBC, also realized there would never be a better time to strike a deal.

As they moved among the classical Georgian facades of the City, the negotiators were determined to hammer out an agreement, figuratively looking over their shoulders at the looming shadows of Dr McLoughlin and his sidekick, who were prepared to throw the winterers' support to whichever side would give them most leverage. Ellice chaired the crucial discussions but it was Simon McGillivray and Andrew Colvile who cut the final deal. "Simon Pure and I," exulted the triumphant Bay Committeeman, "settled it in a quarter of an hour.... We retain the power of management and get paid for our stolen goods, and they kiss the rod."

The twelve-thousand-word contract, signed March 26, 1821, was a complex and sophisticated document, but its effect was simple. When one of the NWC winterers finished reading it, he looked up from its convoluted clauses and exclaimed: "Amalgamation? This isn't amalgamation but submersion. We are drowned men!" Certainly, the HBC's seventy-seven shareholders had little to complain about – particularly since their stock moved up 100 percent with news of the merger.

The contract was to be effective for twenty-one years, commencing in 1821; its multiple provisions provided for amalgamation of the Hudson's Bay Company and North West Company assets, each valued at £200,000. The new business would clearly be operating under the HBC name and Charter. A joint board established to advise on management of the fur trade included Ellice and Simon McGillivray, but it was dominated by Bay Committeemen and the stock split guaranteed control by the HBC. "The union of the North West and Hudson's Bay companies created an enterprise of power unequalled in the history of the fur trade," concluded John S. Galbraith, the pre-eminent American scholar of British Empire history.

William McGillivray and his family.

While the new HBC flourished, many of the senior NWC partners did not. The hard-won terms of amalgamation stayed in place for barely three years. In 1824 the original profit-sharing agreement was abrogated and under the new arrangement the former NWC agency partners were issued common stock – and thereby lost their votes and their influence in the HBC's affairs. Worse, they had to put up a bond of £50,000 to meet the many legal claims being made against their former partnership. Just how far their fortunes had sunk became clear when William McGillivray died on October 16, 1825, leaving Simon to satisfy the family's mounting debts. The surviving brother promptly declared bankruptcy; the McGillivrays' creditors eventually received only ten shillings on the pound. A vanquished Simon McGillivray fled to Mexico, where he found employment as a "gold commissioner."

The North West Company, that defiant alliance of voyageurs and Highlanders whose audacity established Canada's first indigenous national enterprise, vanished overnight. "The feudal state of Fort William," elegized Washington Irving, "is at an end; its council chamber is silent and desolate; its banquet-hall no longer echoes to the auld-world ditty; the lords of the lakes and the forests are all passed away." What endured was an invigorated Hudson's Bay Company, poised to embark on its golden age.

The monopoly had been legally strengthened and geographically expanded by Lord Bathurst, as his promised reward for the merger, through an Act of Parliament passed on July 2, 1821. For an annual token payment of five shillings, the new organization was granted control, renewable in twenty-one years, over the whole of British North America except for the colonies already occupying the Atlantic shore and the St Lawrence-Lower Great Lakes area. Sir Alexander Mackenzie's twenty-year-old dream of a transcontinental trading empire, extending beyond Rupert's Land, across the Rocky and Coast mountains to the edge of thè Pacific and into Oregon Country, had finally come true. What the Company needed was an Overseas Governor who would fulfil the potential of the Company's new empire.

In 1820 George Simpson, while still in his early thirties, became heir apparent to the HBC's overseas operations. Simpson had no background in the complexities of the fur trade or any demonstrable qualities to assume such burdensome responsibilites. Instead, he was chosen because he had not been tainted by the internecine warfare of the previous decade, because he could bring to the Company the counting-house mentality it needed, and because he carried himself with that manner of self-confident authority the circumstances demanded. Simpson had been appointed at the culmination of tensions between the HBC and NWC. Although London-trained, he was Scottish-bred and that allowed him to deal effectively with the proud Highlanders in charge of the North West operations.

George Simpson in the 1820s.

Born out of wedlock to an unknown mother and the wastrel son of a Calvinist minister, he had been raised mainly by his aunt in the northern county of Ross-shire. Having shown promise in mathematics at school, young George was offered an apprenticeship by his uncle, Geddes Mackenzie Simpson, at his London sugar brokerage, Graham & Simpson, a partnership that expanded in 1812 to include Andrew Colvile. Simpson impressed his seniors enough that his nomination by Colvile in 1820 as acting Governor-in-Chief of Rupert's Land and possible replacement for Overseas Governor William Williams was unanimously accepted. Thus began a lifelong alliance between two men of different backgrounds and generations. "To you," Simpson later wrote to Colvile, "I feel that I am solely indebted for my advancement in Life...." After plunging briefly into the fracas of the Athabasca fur trade against the Nor'Westers, Simpson was given command of the new Northern Department.

In that capacity, the as yet untested Simpson called together the Chief Factors and Chief Traders of the Northern Department for their first meeting. Over the portages and trails they trickled in from every quadrant of the extended Hudson's Bay empire. Deep in the summer of 1821, the triumphant traders of the Company of Adventurers and the vanquished wintering partners of the now-defunct North West Company converged on York Factory.

The two groups eyed each other with deep suspicion, the gaunt cast of their weather-ravaged faces and their self-conscious gestures reflecting the tensions of the occasion. But the lavish courses of venison pie, roast partridge, basted wild duck and grilled Arctic char, washed down with generous refills of sherry and old port, soon had their mellowing effect. The feast, so carefully choreographed by the wily Simpson, developed into a garrulous mutual admiration society. They began to compare notes, laughing at how they might have bested each other in this or that confrontation. By dawn both groups were swearing allegiance to one another – and to Simpson, their newly acknowledged leader.

A bastard by birth and by persuasion, George Simpson dominated the HBC during the next four crucial decades. He was one of the few men who lived up to his own Napoleonic pretensions, ruling an empire larger than any in the French emperor's most fanciful dreams. A painting of Napoleon decorated the anteroom of Simpson's office. And like his idol, the wilderness autocrat laid claim to uncommon privilege that was nurtured by the obsequiousness of lieutenants in the field deferring to his certitudes. In height and in bearing he even resembled the "Little Emperor."

The most capable field marshal the HBC ever had, Simpson achieved the daunting task of re-establishing the Company's monopoly after decades of fierce competition with the Nor'Westers. By 1826 Simpson was officially Governor of both the Northern and Southern departments. Masterminding the thin vanguard of Bay functionaries, Simpson acted with the lordly hauteur of a man in charge of his private universe. He ranged across his domain in furiously paced forays, inspecting his posts, hectoring discouraged Factors, preaching "OEconomy" – his Draconian version of cost-cutting – and loving every minute of it. While the Governor's inspection tours set speed and endurance records that have never been beaten (or even attempted), there was time for pomp in lieu of circumstance. Simpson's party, which usually included an escorting canoe or two, would put in to shore just before entering any settlement to give the Governor time to don his beaver topper and his paddlers a moment to spruce up in their best shirts. Ready and set, they would sweep towards the fort's tiny log dock at top speed. Once within sight and sound of the HBC fort, the performance would begin. A bugler, an occasional bagpiper and the

George Simpson's oversized express canoe at Fort William.

voices of his chanting paddlers would blend into a grand orchestration announcing the birchbark Napoleon's arrival.

Despite such lordly trappings, Simpson was more of a viceroy, in that he ruled his province only as the representative of an external sovereign power. For the first thirty years of Simpson's term, the London Governor in charge was Sir John Henry Pelly, who consolidated the Hudson's Bay Company status within the British financial establishment. Andrew Colvile, Simpson's original mentor, served as HBC Deputy Governor from 1839 to 1852, when he succeeded Pelly as Governor.

Simpson's success in extending the Company's Rupert's Land monopoly in every direction, staving off possible rivals to replace the Nor'westers while pushing HBC monetary returns to unprecedented levels, was in large part due to the calibre of his carefully chosen lieutenants.

The wildest shores of George Simpson's trading estate were the HBC's Columbia and New Caledonia departments, stretching from the Gulf of California to the southern edge of Alaska. The Company's Pacific affairs, while ultimately governed by the whims and dictates of Simpson acting on behalf of the HBC's London Committee, were in the hands of a defiant triumvirate of Galahads: Dr John McLoughlin, Peter Skene Ogden and Sir James Douglas, former Nor'Westers all, who ruled their distant provinces with unorthodox methods and astounding results.

The territories south and east of the Columbia River, which Simpson realized might one day be claimed by the United States, were trapped clean in a deliberate scorched-earth tactic meant to confound the American mountain men infiltrating Simpson's empire. Peter Skene Ogden led six forays between 1824 and 1830 into the Snake River's immense drainage basin, a convoluted land

Sir James Douglas, the first governor of British Columbia.

of unclimbed mountains and torrential streams stretching from Wyoming (its source) to the northwest corner of Utah, northeastern Nevada, much of Idaho and slices of what are now the states of Oregon and Washington. Bolstered by his combative nature, Ogden faced brutal challenges and survived them all. Besides trapping thousands of beaver, and having to outwit rampaging mountain men and hostile Indians to stay alive, he became the first white man to explore much of the area.

The lieutenant Simpson chose for the Columbia Department in the potentially explosive Oregon Country was six-foot-four John McLoughlin, a striking figure with a shock of shoulder-length white hair. From his headquarters at Fort Vancouver on Oregon's Columbia River, Chief Factor McLoughlin ruled for two decades – from 1824 to 1845 – with such benevolent effectiveness that he was posthumously accorded the title "Father of Oregon."

The HBC's interests flourished under McLoughlin, but the Chief Factor inevitably succeeded in rousing Simpson's ire. Unlike Simpson, who regarded himself primarily as a colonial administrator, tough and efficient but only marginally concerned with the welfare of the people and land where the HBC operated, McLoughlin felt he was in the process of founding a new society. Given the choice between fattening the Company's balance sheets and acting according to the dictates of his conscience, he opted for the latter.

The strain developed mainly over McLoughlin's generous treatment of potential American settlers and disagreement over whether emphasis was to be placed on ships or trading posts in developing Company business along the Pacific. McLoughlin favoured a chain of permanent posts that would monopolize pelt supplies the year round; Simpson opted for the use of ships and appointed his kinsman Aemilius Simpson head of a new marine department. The dispute between the two climaxed as a result of Simpson's mishandling of the investigation of the murder of McLoughlin's son in the territory. A bitterly indignant McLoughlin soon quit his post and the Company's West Coast pursuits passed into the hands of James Douglas.

When it became apparent that the 49th parallel would become the international boundary between British territories under the HBC and the American territories, Douglas was ordered to oversee construction of a new post on Vancouver Island. He examined many a potential site before settling on the location for the HBC installation, named Fort Victoria. "The place itself appears to be a perfect 'Eden'..." Douglas wrote to a friend in 1843. From his Eden, Douglas, a mulatto of elegant mien whose character was a perplexing combination of endearing romanticism and glacial tenacity, guided British Columbia's metamorphosis from savage fur farm to British colony to Canadian province and played a dominant role in all three incarnations.

With this Pacific empire forged by Ogden, McLoughlin and Douglas guarding the southern and western flanks of Simpson's domain, he entrusted the northern flank to Dr John Rae, sent "to delineate the Northern Shores from the Straits of the Fury and Hecla."

"An idea has entered my head," the Governor wrote Rae on May 11, 1844, "that you are one of the fittest men in the country to conduct an Expedition for the purpose of completing the survey of the Northern Coast. As regards the management of the people and endurance of toil, either in walking, boating or starving, I think you are better adapted for this work than most of the gentn. with whom I am acquainted."

A wilderness physician, ardent naturalist and professional iconoclast, Rae would become the HBC's most accomplished and most controversial northern explorer. He led four Arctic expeditions, walking an incredible 23,000 miles. Unlike the earlier pioneers of Samuel Hearne's vintage, who entered the primaeval wilderness as supercargo on Indian voyages, Rae was an exuberant solo adventurer of almost boyish enthusiasm who had picked up the Eskimos' techniques for scavenging food in a savage land. Yet his Arctic journeys were scientifically planned, moving the Company's trade frontier out of the thinning beaver swamps of the south into the Arctic watershed. His meticulous delineation of the eastern portion of the North West Passage came closest to fulfilling the original impulse that had led so many explorers to batter their vessels and themselves against the brute force of the wind and ice – among them Sir John Franklin, who led a doomed 1845-48 search for a North West Passage.

Dr John Rae in 1858.

Despite Rae's virile triumphs (and, more likely, because of them), he was disparaged by some contemporaries as indiscreet, mercenary and arrogant. Such charges were based mainly on his 1854 trip into the North, when he met Eskimos who sold him artifacts abandoned by members of Franklin's expedition, providing the first word since their disappearance of the horrendous circumstances of their final days: that they had indulged in cannibalism to keep themselves alive a bit longer.

The shocking news of the find mesmerized the civilized world but caused unexpected abuse to be heaped on Rae. He was accused of not following up Eskimo tales to double-check their authenticity and of rushing back to London to claim the £10,000 reward for having discovered the fate of the Franklin expedition. Where was the proof of cannibalism among the crewmen? Surely, it was said, the piety, the courage, the utter *Britishness* of the men would never have permitted such an outrage. (Documentation of the cannibalism first reported by Rae didn't come until the early 1980s, when Dr Owen Beattie, a physical anthropologist at the University of Alberta, located and studied skeletal remains still recognizable as belonging to Franklin's sailors. As well as evidence of scurvy and lead poisoning possibly due to faulty canning of meat carried by the ships, he found "fracture lines [indicating] that the skull had been forcibly broken," and marks on the right femur that "were most likely knife marks." "The head, arms and legs, easily portable," Beattie concluded, were "carried along as a food supply.")

Rae's remarkable exploits ended with his early retirement, probably the result of physical exhaustion. The last of the HBC's great pathfinders, Rae had assured Simpson his northern flank. With the periphery of the HBC's land empire secure, the viceroy was able to concentrate on rebuilding the HBC's fur monopoly inside Rupert's Land.

Evidence that the fur trade was flourishing was best represented by Simpson's favourite trader, John Rowand, Chief Factor of Edmonton House. A key conduit in the trade because of its location on the North Saskatchewan River, Edmonton, under Rowand's command, quickly became the most productive fort in the Territories. A vital trading centre for tribes in the Plains group (the Assiniboine, Cree, Blackfoot, Sarcee, Gros Ventre, Peigan and Blood), the hexagonal enclosures at Edmonton soon sprouted a dozen warehouses, residences and workshops. The most imposing structure of all was Rowand's own "Big House" – known to the locals as Rowand's Folly – a three-storey residence and office that boasted the Northwest's first glass windows and only ballroom.

John Rowand stood even shorter than Simpson but was known as the Big Mountain for good reason; his ample girth was supported by equally outrageous quantities of bombast and bluster. His renowned and feared temper made even Simpson seem a bit of a milquetoast. On one occasion, when he and the Catholic missionary Albert Lacombe were out riding across the plains, they were resting at a campfire when they suddenly found themselves surrounded by two hundred Blackfoot, clearly on the warpath. Rowand marched up to the chief and roared, "*Stop, you villains!*" – then turned his back and resumed his meal. Recognizing his opponent, the chief not only called off the raiding party but was so abject in his apologies that according to the bagpiper Colin Fraser, who reported the incident, many of the Indians "actually cried

(continued on page 150)

JOHN RAE AND THE FRANKLIN EXPEDITION

"Where is Franklin?" was the question that pre-occupied Victorian England at mid-century. In 1845 with two lavishly equipped ships, 139 men and three years' worth of provisions, Sir John Franklin had left for the Arctic determined to claim the North West Passage for Great Britain. By 1847, when no word of the expedition's whereabouts had been received, the British Admiralty dispatched four search parties, but they failed to find any trace of Franklin or his

(Right) Sir John Franklin with (below) an imagined view of his ships the Erebus *and the* Terror *beset by ice at Beechey Island in 1846.*

crew. Public opinion, spurred on by the tireless lobbying of Lady Franklin, demanded an answer to the mystery. The summer of 1850 saw nine more rescue vessels butting into the pack ice of Lancaster Sound. (Between 1847 and 1859 there were to be thirty-two unsuccessful search expeditions in all.)

While surveying the northern reaches of the Company's holdings on the Boothia Peninsula in April of 1854, the HBC surgeon and mapmaker Dr John Rae met an Eskimo wearing a gold-braid naval cap band. In questioning him, Rae heard of a party of white men who had starved to death near a large river a long distance off. From further conversations with Eskimos, Rae reconstructed the final days of

(Opposite) These illustrations reconstructing the movements of Franklin's party were first published in an 1860 report by Leopold McClintock. (Below) Crewmen cutting ice near the embedded ships in 1847. (Inset, top) Abandoning ship. (Middle) Dragging heavy sleds and whaleboats, the survivors head for the nearest HBC post 870 miles south. (Bottom) In 1859 McClintock's men found two skeletons by a boat on King William Island.
(Left) An 1862 portrait of John Rae in Arctic garb.
(Below) This painting by Charles F. Comfort shows Rae with Eskimos at Pelly Bay in 1854 receiving a silver spoon bearing the crest and initials of Francis Crozier, Sir John Franklin's second-in-command.

Franklin's men, including their desperate resort to cannibalism before the last of them died of scurvy and starvation in a wretched encampment near the mouth of Back's Great Fish River. Unable to go there because the summer's thaw ruled out sledding, Rae returned to York Factory and sailed for England with forty-five relics of the Franklin expedition purchased from the Eskimos, including Sir John's Order of Merit and a silver plate engraved with his name.

The Admiralty was satisfied with Rae's conclusions but a suspicious public and Franklin's implacable widow were not. On July 1, 1857, a small party financed by Lady Franklin under the command of Royal Navy Captain Leopold McClintock set sail for the Arctic. A message they found nearly two years later in a rock cairn on King William Island filled in the missing pieces of the puzzle. Scrawled around the borders of a routine "all's well" report from 1847 was a second message dated April 25, 1848. It reported that Franklin had died on June 11, 1847, and that the 105 remaining officers and men had abandoned their ice-locked ships. In the upper right, an ominous postscript had been penned, "and start on tomorrow 26th for Back's Fish River."

FRANKLIN RELICS BROUGHT BY DR RAE.

(Above) A selection of the relics Rae handed over to the Admiralty included watch pieces, knives and Franklin's monogrammed silverware.
(Right) Three of the early casualties of the Franklin expedition were buried on Beechey Island in 1846. When examined 138 years later by University of Alberta anthropologist Dr. Owen Beattie, the bodies in these graves had been kept in a near-perfect state of preservation by the Arctic permafrost.

JOHN TORRINGTON, A.B.   JOHN HARTNELL, A.B.   WILLIAM BRAINE, R.M.

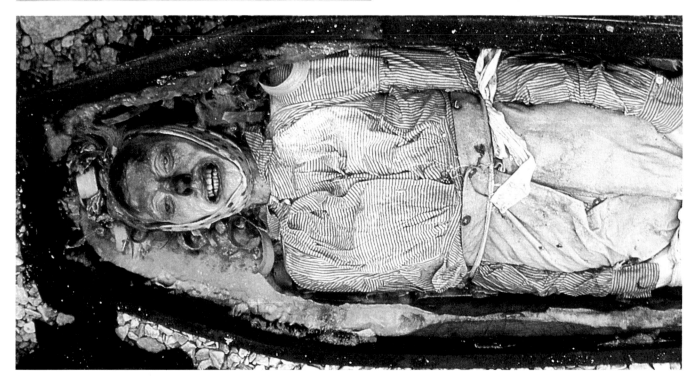

(Left) This multilingual form, with its two handwritten messages, is the only surviving document of the Franklin expedition. McClintock's men discovered it inside a tin cylinder after (below) dismantling a cairn at Victory Point on King William Island. The final message is upside down on the top right corner of the page. (Bottom) Autopsies of twenty-two-year-old John Torrington and his two crew mates revealed that lead poisoning from poorly soldered tin cans had played a significant role in their doom.

with vexation." Under Rowand, Edmonton's importance to the Company was counted both in terms of its impressive fur catch and its production of pemmican and York boats.

By the middle of the nineteenth century, Simpson and his lieutenants had staved off all incursions to the HBC's monopoly while ensuring the Company a quarter century of unparalleled prosperity. The most dangerous threat should in theory have been the agitation for annexation of HBC lands by leaders of public opinion in the Canadian provinces. There was no shortage of windy political rhetoric on the issue, and George Brown, the founding editor of the Toronto *Globe*, wrote thunderous editorials claiming that only the extension of Canada's borders westward to the Pacific would revive the colony's stagnant economy. But there was little response. The politicians were all too aware of the inadequacy of their treasuries; taking on the administrative cost of the huge HBC territories seemed neither desirable nor realistic.

Then, with the suddenness of a summer storm, this standoffish attitude changed. The realization struck home that if nothing was done, Red River and what would someday become the Canadian heartland might be annexed by the United States. Once again, the Adventurers' empire was under siege.

YORK BOATS

Called York boats because their most common destination was York Factory, George Simpson started replacing canoes with these vessels throughout the HBC's empire after he became Governor. A clumsy vessel in some ways, the motivation for introducing them was, as with so much of what Simpson did, economy — they carried more than three times the payload of the largest birchbark canoes.

First built at Albany Fort in the 1740s, the York boat was based on an old Orkney design that in turn derived from Viking longships. Flat-bottomed, its pointed bow and

(Below) An artist's impression of York boats arriving at Norway House. Such fleets were referred to as "brigades." (Overleaf) Paul Kane's Brigade of Boats *was based on sketches first done while he was travelling with an HBC York boat brigade.*

stern angled upwards at forty-five degrees, making it easy to beach or backwater off a sandbar.

Two skilled workmen could put together a York boat in two weeks. Special care was taken to select a piece of spruce or tamarack that, when carved into a keel, could withstand the stresses of running rapids and repeated beachings. The rest of the boat was knocked together out of spruce planking, overlapped to make the hull watertight, then coated with pitch.

Propelled by six or eight oarsmen working twenty-foot oars, a York boat underway had little of the canoe's grace. To row it, the oarsmen would rise from their seats, bracing themselves with one foot, then pull back on the oar, sitting down again in the process. Steering was done with a long oar mounted at the stern and a bowman kept a lookout for rocks and other obstacles. For open water, the York boat was equipped with a large square sail, which also served as a tent at night.

One place where York boats were at a distinct disadvantage compared to canoes was at portages. Because of their size and weight, York boats had to be hauled along on log rollers, with the crew, serving as beasts of burden, straining away in harness.

As pioneers flooded the west, York boats began to carry more

and more general cargo for their use. Among the more unusual items they transported were the bells for St Boniface Cathedral in Winnipeg and the first piano in the Red River Colony.

The last York boat brigade arrived in York Factory in 1871, and as that fort declined in importance, so did the York boats. They were still, however, used at more isolated posts for quite some time, and the last commercial York boat was built

at Norway House in 1924. Today in Manitoba, smaller versions of the York boat can still be seen, used now for racing in the summer.

(Opposite) Portaging York boats. Upon the arrival of a brigade of York boats at a portage (top), the first stage in portaging was to remove all the freight from the boats (middle). The emptied boats were then pulled onto land and hauled across the portage on log rollers (bottom) using human

power. Because York boats were much larger than canoes, they couldn't use the old portage paths and special, wider trails had to be cleared for them. At certain busy portages, the boats' cargoes, once unloaded, were transported on Red River carts drawn by oxen.
(Above) The sternman in a modern racing York boat at Norway House in Manitoba. The York boat's long steering oar may be a legacy from its ancestor, the Viking longboat.

155

CHAPTER NINE

THE COMPANY THAT BECAME A NATION

SIMPSON WAS SUMMONED TO BUCKINGHAM PALACE IN 1841 to become Sir George. There is no first-hand record of his knighthood ceremony but it would have been a grand occasion, for the young Queen Victoria had set herself the task of restoring both the splendour and popularity of the monarchy. The past triumphs of Lord Nelson and the Duke of Wellington had made England the leader among nations; the Royal Navy patrolled three oceans ready to sink unbelievers at a moment's notice; a burgeoning London was the centre of world commerce and culture, and the Empire was being touted as an instrument of Christian destiny.

It was a splendid time to be a member of the British gentry and Simpson had just been initiated into its golden circle. The knighthood itself and the continuing prosperity of the Company under his leadership were soon to alter his outlook permanently. Gone was the wilderness administrator; the Governor now ranked himself a diplomat and international financier.

His triumphant 1841-42 world tour – from London, via Halifax, Boston, Montreal, Fort Vancouver, California, Hawaii, Alaska, Siberia and Europe – only served to increase his stature.

The Company was in a state of near euphoria. Its Rupert's Land monopoly had been successfully extended in every direction; no significant rivals had replaced the Nor'Westers; American settlers had not yet captured the Oregon Country; the monetary returns of the Company's operations had never been higher; and its Governor and his Committeemen had Britain's leading politicians in their pockets. If only it could have lasted.

. It didn't. American expansionists were mobilized by their discovery that steam could redraw the map of the continent. Although a few short "portage" rail lines were built in the Canadian provinces during the 1830s and 1840s, the first really major rail project was the Grand Trunk, completed in 1859 between Lévis, Quebec, and Sarnia, Ontario. In contrast, American entrepreneurs had been pushing steel across their country at a much

(Opposite) Sir George Simpson in the late 1850s.

faster pace; by 1860, thirty thousand route-miles of track had been laid. Any territory not accessible to chuffing locomotives was being exploited by steamboats, the belching paddle-wheelers that were turning the Missouri and Mississippi into riverine freeways. Minnesota, just south of the original Selkirk grant, had attained statehood by 1858, becoming a nest of 150,000 expansion-minded citizens.

These and other stirrings prompted Canada West patriots to rally against the possibility of Red River annexation and, eventually, against the monopoly of the Hudson's Bay Company itself. The early Canadian capitalists, especially the competition-conscious owners of the lumber and grist mills, began to express their revulsion at this foreign, feudal and forbidding enterprise, which, as a petition from the Toronto Board of Trade complained, "assumed the power to enact tariffs, collect custom dues, and levy taxes against British subjects, and has enforced unjust and arbitrary laws in defiance of every principle of right and justice."

Having taken its mandate for granted for nearly two centuries, the HBC now faced a fierce and widespread challenge to its hegemony: a wave of populist sentiment that viewed its monopoly (renewed in 1838 by the British government for a further twenty-one years) as the chief obstacle to dreams of free trade, settlement and transcontinental nationhood.

At Red River, a much more subtle undercurrent festering with racial, social and religious resentments was changing the character of the settlement and its people. The most jarring disruption to the Colony's stability had been the arrival of Frances, Simpson's British bride. Distinctions of class and parentage that had largely been ignored during a generation of HBC and NWC occupancy

Lower Fort Garry. Governor George Simpson had the "Stone Fort," as it became known, built to serve as his headquarters in the Fur Country.

suddenly surfaced to upend family and community equilibrium. "There is a strange revolution in the manners of the country," noted James Douglas. "Indian wives were at one time the vogue, the half breed supplanted these, and now we have the lovely tender exotic torn from its parent bed...."

The roots of these changes had been planted long before. After the death of Lord Serlkirk, the languishing colony's presence provided living proof of the HBC's charter rights, yet nearly every active Bay man resented its intrusive influence on the fur trade. In 1836, the Selkirk family had moved to rid itself of the unhappy land asset by selling it back to the HBC for stock worth £84,000, which in due time brought returns many times the late Earl's losses. Despite a severe flood in 1826, the settlement had grown, with imported livestock, new grist mills and the continued buffalo hunt providing the chief economic mainstays. Its population had mushroomed from fewer than 300 in 1818 to 4,369 by 1840 and, by mid-century, 12,000 acres had been settled.

Red River continued to expand not only geographically but socially, sprouting five distinct communities. One was comprised of the Scots of Kildonan, the brave remnants of the original Selkirk immigrants. Nearby lived the retired Hudson's Bay factors and their families, who quickly became the settlement's self-appointed

COUNTRY WIVES

A "country wife" was what the Bay men called the Indian women they lived with while in the Fur Country. Although some were virtual slaves, sold in barter for trade goods, genuine love matches were quite frequent, too.

Country wives were common, and increasingly tolerated by the Company, right into the nineteenth century, although mixed-race women later became the preferred brides. What finally ended the custom was the arrival at Red River in 1830 of George Simpson's English bride Frances. Overnight she created a fashion for white, church-wed wives.

(Left) Alfred Jacob Miller's The Trapper's Bride *presents a rather romanticized view of the obtaining of a country wife.*
(Right) Lady Douglas. Of mixed ancestry, she became Sir James Douglas's country wife at sixteen, his legal wife thirteen years later.
(Below) The Governor of Red River and his English-bred lady.

leaders. To the south and west of the river junction lived the Métis of the Upper Settlement and White Horse Plain, the most dynamic element in the region, increasingly militant in their aspirations to control their own destinies. Finally, there were the villages of the Swampy Cree in St Peter's, above the Red River Delta, and the band of Saulteaux at Baie St Paul, up the Assiniboine.

The HBC had never generated much loyalty among its employees at Red River. Because Simpson preferred to recruit his new officers in Scotland, he promoted few if any Métis. One exception was Cuthbert Grant, leader of the death squad that had savaged the HBC's settlers at Seven Oaks a decade earlier, who resurfaced in 1828 as Simpson's Warden of the Plains. Grant's main function was to co-opt the rebellious spirit of the Métis and this he achieved, at least temporarily – but neither Simpson nor Grant could hold back the forces gathering to engulf the settlement.

An impromptu free-trade movement in furs developed as independent traders began to move both ways across the international boundary. The fragile equilibrium of the situation was shattered in 1843 when Norman Wolfred Kittson, an emigrant Lower Canadian serving with the American Fur Company, opened a trading post at Pembina in North Dakota, about seventy miles south of Fort Garry. His instructions were to capture the Red River fur trade and he set about it with energy and cunning, drawing many of the independents into his orbit. By the late 1840s, free traders had infiltrated so much of the commerce that Simpson realized the continued existence of the Red River Colony was at stake. Using the threat of American incursion as their fulcrum and lever, the London Committee persuaded the British government to dispatch three companies (340 men) of the 6th Regiment of Foot (the Royal Warwickshires) to maintain the peace. The presence of the soldiers provided a deterrent to free trade, but after two years their place had been taken by a dubious rabble of fifty-six British Army pensioners under the command of Major William Caldwell, who was also appointed Governor of Assiniboia.

The agitation for free trade, which had languished during the pacifying interlude of the Warwickshires, came alive with a vengeance, and Kittson's voluminous take of furs was threatening to dominate the trade. Using the flimsy excuse that Caldwell's appointment had separated local governing authority from the Company's influence, HBC Chief Factor John Ballenden arrested an outspoken Mixed Blood named Pierre-Guillaume Sayer and three other Métis on charges of illegal trafficking in pelts. Ballenden never questioned that a proper verdict would be returned, reinstating the Company's monopoly. He was wrong, at least in so far as the verdict was understood by the three hundred Métis who gathered to hear Jean-Louis Riel, an ardent Métis nationalist whose first-born and namesake would become the patron saint of Canadian rebels. Riel exhorted them to liberate Sayer and assert freedom of trade for the New Nation.

Sayer was in due course found guilty of trading furs but the jurors went further. They also recommended mercy "as it appeared that he thought he had a right to trade as he and others were under the impression that there was a free trade." Chief Factor Ballenden committed the strategic error of unthinkingly accepting this hybrid verdict and then compounded his mistake by setting Sayer and his co-defendants free on the spot.

As the doors of the courtroom opened and Sayer stepped into the sunshine, Riel and his troops came to the instant (and as it turned out, irrevocable) conclusion that their fellow Métis had been acquitted, and that the fur trade had officially been set free. "*Vive la Liberté! Le commerce est libre!*" went the victory shouts. Musket-fire exploded skyward as the exhilarated Métis rode out to spread the news that the HBC's monopoly had been broken at last.

It was becoming increasingly clear that either the Canadian or the British government would have to take decisive action against the HBC's Charter.

By the 1850s, Sir George Simpson must have been aware, however reluctant he may have been to admit it, that his swath of absolute power could no longer hold men or causes. In his mid-sixties, the coils of wrath that characterized his youth having retreated deep inside him, he assumed the mantle of the fur trade's elder statesman and turned his attention to profitable investments on his own account. The overseas Governor's burden had been reduced somewhat by the appointment in January 1849 of Andrew Colvile's son Eden as Associate Governor of Rupert's Land. Simpson still sallied forth on his annual inspection tours, but they had evolved into theatrical processions, staged more for show than for commercial purpose. Simpson's actual responsibilities focussed mainly on lobbying in London and in Montreal to keep the politicians aware of why the Company and its royal Charter still ought to be accorded such extraordinary privileges.

Almost by instinct, a group of settlers met to form a committee that could monitor the Company's actions and safeguard their own interests. It was not a powerful or even representative group, but the Assiniboia Committee organized the settlers' anti-HBC campaign which rapidly accelerated where it really mattered – in London, among the British politicians and bureaucrats who would soon be responsible for dealing with the Company's request that its licence be again renewed, in May of 1859. Late in the summer of 1856, Simpson had warned the London Committee that the Company was "...in a very critical position, the authorities being overawed by the numerical strength of the Halfbreed race; so that, at any moment an unpopular measure or accidental collision might lead to a general rising against the Company and the destruction of their establishments. In the meantime, by tact and forbearance, we contrive to maintain the peace and are making large returns – a state of things which may continue one, two or more years, although at all times liable to be interrupted suddenly."

The issue came to a head when, the following year, Henry Labouchere (afterwards Lord Taunton), Secretary of State for the Colonies in Lord Palmerston's first administration, called for a Select Committee of the House of Commons to investigate the case for renewing the HBC's trading monopoly, and appointed himself its chairman. Among that august body's nineteen members were some of the notables of British politics at the time. Edward "Bear" Ellice would act throughout the hearings as the Company's counsel for the defence.

And so the Hudson's Bay Company and its Charter were at last put on trial. The committee sat eighteen times and cross-examined twenty-five witnesses (Simpson among them), asking 6,098 questions; the transcript of its hearings covers 450 pages. "The disclosures laid bare by this accumulation of testimony, letters, petitions, memorials and other evidence produced before the Parliamentary Select Committee, made the deepest kind of a public sensation," wrote Gustavus Myers in his *History of Canadian Wealth*. "For nearly two centuries the Hudson's Bay Company had represented itself in England as the grand evangel of religion, colonization, and civilization among the Indians; for nearly two centuries it had assiduously spread abroad its pretended reputation; and by insisting long enough upon its assumed virtues had been credited with them by the large mass of the unknowing. Now the truth was revealed, and bad as it was, yet it was regarded as undoubtedly only part of the whole. Imminently threatened, as the Hudson's Bay Company now was, with judicial and legislative extinction, it had to adopt some hurried expedient to save itself."

That expedient proved to be the last witness produced before the committee adjourned to write its report. He was Ellice, then in his mid-seventies but still respected by the parliamentarians and very much a force within the HBC's governing councils. He had been associated with the Canadian fur trade for half a century and, after a rambling lecture on its historical importance, he electrified the committee with his reply to the chairman's question: Would

The Simpson home at Lachine, near Montreal.

it be difficult to make an arrangement between the Canadian Government and the Company for the extension of settlement into Hudson's Bay territory?

Canoes assembled for the spectacle put on by Simpson for the visiting Prince of Wales.

"Not only would there be no difficulty in it," replied the Bear, as if on cue, "but the Hudson's Bay Company would be [only] too glad to make a cession of any part of that territory for the purpose of settlement, upon one condition, that Canada shall bear the expense of governing it and maintaining a good police and preventing the introduction, so far as they can, of competition within the fur trade."

As the result of Ellice's statement, the committee's report was a foregone conclusion. As if by magic, the future of the Canadian West had suddenly become negotiable. The committee's majority recommendations, though mildly phrased, were hard-boiled in their intent: the Company must surrender its claims to Vancouver Island immediately and to the mainland (where a colony was to be created) soon afterwards; the Red River and Saskatchewan districts were to be annexed eventually to Canada; only those portions of the Indian territory considered unsuitable for settlement were to remain under the HBC's monopoly control for another twenty-one years. The Company of Adventurers could no longer claim, as it had in the original Charter, to be the "true and absolute Lordes and Proprietors" of the land beyond the westering sea.

Walking in the sibilant rain falling on the granite blocks of the Lachine Canal, an aged Sir George Simpson must have reflected on this remarkable shift, and on how alone he had become. His wife Frances, and McLoughlin, Ogden, Rowand, Pelly and many others who had shared his life, were dead. Somehow it didn't seen fair they had all abandoned him. Like a latter-day King Lear, raging against his own mortality, Simpson was now dragging himself painfully across the land he had once ruled.

His last days, however, were enlivened by a distinguished visitor, the Prince of Wales, an awkward eighteen-year-old who was to become the future Edward VII. To give him a special treat, Simpson decided to assemble a grand canoe reception on the St Lawrence: a flotilla of ten birchbark voyageur canoes, their HBC flags flapping in the summer wind, each manned by twelve Iroquois in full regalia of red flannel shirts, blue trousers and round caps decorated with dyed feathers pretending to be ostrich plumes. That day in the sun with the future king turned out to be Sir George Simpson's formal farewell. Only two days later, still flushed with the exhilaration of the royal occasion, the Governor was stricken with apoplexy. By the morning of September 7, 1860, he was dead.

Without the great wilderness viceroy to defend its empire, the Company's grip on Rupert's Land began to slip. Realizing that neither Canada nor England would invest the capital required to colonize Rupert's Land, the British Colonial Secretary, the Duke of Newcastle, directed his efforts to the private sector, particularly to the British financiers eager to build a railway and telegraph system across the upper part of North America.

Enter Edward Watkin, a former British railway manager, who had been hired by two of London's merchant bankers to help resolve the problems of Canada's troubled Grand Trunk Railway, which they had financed. He studied the situation and quickly decided that the best prescription for the Grand Trunk's salvation was to build a railway from the Atlantic to the Pacific. As a first step, he organized the Atlantic and Pacific Postal and Telegraph Company, requesting a ten-mile-wide right-of-way across Rupert's Land for telegraph poles and a wagon road, presumably a precursor of the railway line. On November 17, 1862, the Duke of Newcastle, who heartily endorsed the idea, visited Henry Hulse Berens, then Governor of the HBC, to sound him out on the Watkin proposal.

The twentieth man to hold the office since Prince Rupert of the Rhine, Berens, upholding a staunch family tradition, had spent thirty years gracing the HBC Committee. A director of the Bank of England, his great-grandfather, grandfather and father had each served on the Committee. The Colonial Secretary approached the touchy issue as moderately and gently as he could, presenting the promoter's idea of slashing a strip across the heart of the HBC territory as a patriotic gesture to tie the Empire together. Berens's reply was as indignant as it was emotional. "What?" he blustered. "Sequester our very tap-root? Take away the fertile lands where our buffaloes feed? Let in all kinds of people to squat and settle and frighten away the fur-bearing animals they don't kill and hunt? Im-

possible! Destruction – extinction – of our time-honoured industry…"

That emphatic defence of his turf having been delivered, the
Governor reverted to type and, shrewdly squinting at the Duke,
queried: "If these gentlemen are so patriotic, why don't they buy
us out?"

"What is your price?" calmly inquired the Colonial Secretary.

"Well, about a million and a half."

A sales agreement was concluded on June 15, 1863. To raise the
large amount of cash demanded by the Governor required greater
assets and more risk than were represented by the two bankers
backing Watkin. The financial conglomerate that came up with
the £1,500,000 called itself the International Financial Society.
Incorporated only a month earlier by a consortium of City bankers,
the IFS paid the purring HBC proprietors £300 for each share of
£100 par value, up to the £1.5 million total. The Company was
immediately recapitalized (an elegant term for having its stock
watered) at £2 million, and the shares were sold to the public in
£20 units. Thus the HBC's stock, which had been purchased for
three times its nominal value, had quadrupled in price with no real
change in revenue prospects having taken place. The transactions
left the IFS's owners with a net gain of £300,000; then, having
disposed of its shares, the IFS faded from the scene. For the first
time since the Company's founding in 1670, HBC stock was now
widely distributed among seventeen hundred shareholders, each
one of whom expected a hefty return. *The Times* of July 3, 1863,
called the plan "one of the most important proposals, both in
a financial and national sense, ever introduced on the London
money market."

"Bear" Ellice in his mid-seventies.

Perhaps the only man in London who despaired of the Company's sale to a group of promoters was Edward Ellice. When one
of the IFS negotiators met "the Bear," then bent with age and only
months away from death, in a London arcade, he reported that the
old man had confronted him for some moments without speaking,
in a state of confused abstraction. "Then he passed on, like a man
endeavouring to recollect a long history of difficulty, and to realize
how strangely it had all ended."

The prospectus that had attracted so many eager shareholders
listed the Company's assets at £370,000 in cash; £1,023,500 in
physical plant such as trading posts, ships and offices and 1.4
million square miles, or 896 million acres, of land. "The Southern
District will be opened to European Colonization under a liberal
and systematic scheme of land settlement," spouted the offering
circular. "The Company can, without creating any new and costly

establishments, inaugurate a new policy of colonization and at the same time dispose of mining grants."

That pledge meant very little, but shareholders were reassured by the quality of the new Committeemen who took over the Company's direction. (The only important holdover from the former board was Eden Colvile, whose lengthy tenure and experience at Red River provided essential continuity.) On the Duke of Newcastle's suggestion, Sir Edmund Walker Head was installed as Governor of the reconstituted HBC. He had served as Governor-in-Chief of British North America (1854-61). An Oxford honours graduate in classics, an author, poet and philologist, Head was a thoughtful statesman genuinely concerned with developing Rupert's Land in an orderly fashion, but he soon found himself overwhelmed by Edward Watkin's impatience. The promoter had hurried to Canada as an agent of the new Company and on his own authority had dispatched surveyors into the field.

Head could not condone such outrageous flouting of his authority, particularly since Watkin's own reports made it clear that the Canadian government had expressed no intention of helping finance construction of the telegraph line. The Company did send Dr John Rae, the retired HBC Chief Factor and Arctic explorer, to survey the route, but absence of government support had already killed the project. What the crisis did accomplish was to reactivate Canada's official pressure on the British Colonial Office to resolve the Hudson's Bay territorial dispute. A powerful Canadian delegation arrived at London's Westminster Palace Hotel during October 1868 in a mood for serious bargaining about expropriating the new HBC. The department's files on the issue had been thoroughly studied by Earl Granville, the Colonial Secretary in the Gladstone government, and he had decided to act much more quickly and decisively than any of his predecessors. Correctly divining that the Company and the Canadian delegates would reach their usual impasse, he slapped down in front of both parties on March 9, 1869, a twelve-paragraph ultimatum. The Canadians were the first to capitulate and after that the Company had no choice but to fall into step. Despite loud protests from HBC shareholders, who regarded the Colonial Secretary's terms as a betrayal of their trust, the deal was approved. On November 19, the Hudson's Bay Company signed the Deed of Surrender (which became valid July 15, 1870) and watched its much-coveted monopoly rights evaporate.

While there was no direct charge to the Treasury of the United Kingdom, London did agree to guarantee a loan to the Canadian government of £300,000 (then the equivalent of $1,460,000) that

Sir Edmund Walker Head

was to be the HBC's cash compensation. Among other conditions of the transfer the HBC was allowed to retain:

1. A grant of more than forty-five thousand acres around its 120 existing trading posts. Only four of these forts were in what was then considered to be the fertile belt, but the acreage around Fort Garry alone had immediate cash value.

2. A right to claim, during the ensuing fifty years, blocks of land set out for settlement within its former territory, not to exceed one-twentieth of the fertile area. This grant amounted to seven million acres of some of the best agricultural land in Western Canada.

3. A guarantee of the continuance of its trade without hindrance and with no special taxes or tariffs.

Enemies of the Company interpreted the surrender as the HBC's death blow. "The old lion has been shorn of its mane," one of them gloated, "his roar is no longer heard in the great North-West." The Company's original charter may have been reduced to a decorative parchment, but the HBC was still the largest private landholder in Western Canada and had been handed a rich ransom for relinquishing holdings that, from the Canadian point of view, it ought never to have been allowed to possess. Most significantly, the Company had been relieved of the responsibility of administering those lands just when settlement was promising to make that function dangerous and expensive.

Terms of the sale were routinely ratified by Canada's Parliament and the physical takeover was slated for December 1, 1869. The last meeting of the Northern Department of Rupert's Land was held at Norway House in July 1870. Only seventeen years later, no further commissioned officers were appointed by the HBC and, four years after that, all of the time-honoured titles of the fur trade were withdrawn. But for this one final occasion, the Chief Factors and Chief Traders sat around the great oak table where Sir George Simpson had once ruled and where generations of their predecessors had traded quips and empires. They must have felt as if they were living out the final act in some much-told tale, ordinary men caught in extraordinary circumstances. But the drama was not over.

BAY LIFE
IN THE 1800s

The nineteenth century was a period of severe transition for the Hudson's Bay Company. By its closing decades, the Company had been stripped of its monopoly and had surrendered much of its land. The fur business was also in decline — the beaver hat had been superseded by the silk topper in the 1850s. And although pelts were in demand as fur trim in clothing for instance, the Hudson's Bay Company faced very stiff competition in this market from South American anhinga, the fur of the coypu rat.

But despite these sometimes traumatic changes, life on the Bay, for a common clerk or a factor in the later part of the century, wouldn't have seemed alien to their counterparts one hundred years earlier. The essential fact of life remained the fur trade. True, the trade was not what it had been when the beaver was in great demand, but it was still a money-maker. To exploit the fur business, the Company still required far-flung posts serving large areas — just as it had one hundred years before.

At those posts, something of the old Company discipline still survived. The HBC had abolished its commissioned ranks in 1887, giving up on the idea that it was a land-locked navy, but the gulf between the Factor or Chief Trader and his clerks remained. The Factor's house dominated the post, while the younger unmarried clerks crowded together in a bachelors' hall, just as they had in earlier days.

Weather still defined life in these outposts. While the appearance of the railways in the south had made previously isolated posts such as Fort Garry accessible year-round, northern posts still depended on the rivers and lakes for transportation. At these distant locations, summer remained a time of frenetic activity. Indians came to trade, while furs had to be shipped out and trade goods brought in. In contrast, the winters stretched on with little distraction except tallying up trade goods and furs.

Also unchanged was the sheer, back-breaking toil the fur trade required. The nineteenth century had been an era of great technological innovations, but apart from steam engines to drive ships, these didn't have much effect on the Bay men. Furs still had to be pressed using all the force a half dozen men could muster, and the ninety pound sacks carried in by barges and steamships had to be unloaded by hand. Whatever the changes on a grander level, for the humble Bay men life continued as it had since the earliest days.

(Below) Trade with the Indians was still the central feature of life for the Hudson's Bay Company during the late 1800s. In this sketch of a Company post by Frederic Remington done in the 1890s, a Hudson's Bay Company employee barters with his customers while a Mountie looks on.

Colin Fraser, the trader at Fort Chipewyan in the 1890s, examines his cache of furs. The load here, which included fox, mink and beaver pelts, was valued at more than $35,000.

Taken at Fort Rae in 1895, this photograph shows six Bay men operating a fur press. The purpose of the press was to convert loose furs into tight, manageable bales for transportation.

As a new century dawned at Fort Resolution, things had changed little in one hundred years. Virtually everything, from powering boats to carrying cargo, was done still with human muscle.

(Right) Finished polar bear skins in an HBC fur warehouse today. Although demand for beaver hats dried up in the middle of the nineteenth century, there was, and still remains, a demand for animal pelts.

(Opposite) A musk-ox head used as a towel stand graces an HBC clerk's room in the bachelors' hall at Lower Fort Garry.

(Below) An 1871 picture by the Montreal photographer William Notman shows various chief factors of the Hudson's Bay Company. Notable among them is Chief Commisioner Donald Smith, seated second from left, who became Commisoner and Governor of the Company and, later, Lord Strathcona.

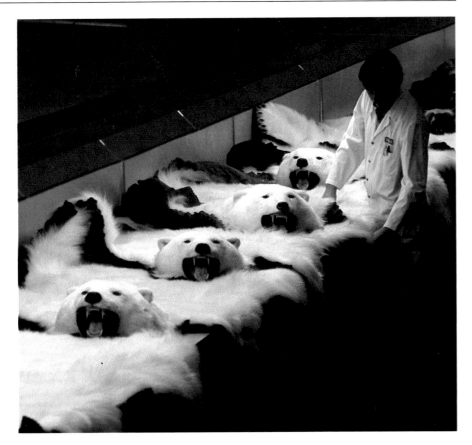

FORT EDMONTON

Perched on a height of land, above the North Saskatchewan River, Fort Edmonton was a key supply point for fur brigades on the plains. During the thirty-year reign of John Rowand as Chief Factor, the fort was one of the most successful HBC posts. Its buildings were smeared with red earth from the area, which when mixed with oil, produced a shade called "durable brown." The most prominent structure was Rowand's "Big House," which had a ballroom that could hold 150 for dinner and dancing and was decorated in a style that artist Paul Kane called "...the most startling, barbaric gaudiness."

(Right) Fort Edmonton as painted by Paul Kane in 1847.
(Above) This 1871 photograph with a reclining frontiersman in front reveals that Kane romanticized the height of the bluff on which the fort is situated.
(Top, left) In 1890 the town of Edmonton is beginning to encircle the old fort, and by 1912 (top, right) it is dwarfed by the new legislature of the province of Alberta.

174

CHAPTER TEN

THE ONCE AND FUTURE EMPIRE

THE LAST OF THE GREAT HISTORICAL FIGURES TO MANI-
pulate the destiny of the Hudson's Bay Company was Donald
A. Smith. Better known as Lord Strathcona, the bearded gentleman in a swallow-tailed coat is now most often pictured in history books doggedly bashing down the last spike of the Canadian
Pacific Railway.

His grandiose financial manoeuvres imbued the lives of many
of his contemporaries with the disquieting sense of overwhelming
inevitability, like facing the first rains of the monsoon season. As
the tattered Smith he spent more than three decades trading furs
deep inside Labrador; as the elegant Strathcona he became a major determining force in the early evolution of Canada's political
economy. His astounding skill as an international financier made
possible the construction of the CPR, a feat that united the country
economically as Confederation had politically. As president of the
Bank of Montreal he headed the largest Canadian financial insti-
tution of its time. Above all, during his four decades in the top
post of the Hudson's Bay Company, he transformed a dominion of
haphazardly linked wilderness posts into an interwoven commercial enterprise.

By dint of having spent nearly half his adult years exiled to
Labrador, the records we have of Smith's appearance are almost
entirely those of his old age. He imagined himself a Viking prince,
the body language of his six-foot frame a lexicon of military preci-
sion. Formidable brows gave his squinting eyes, damaged long ago
by snowblindness, a far-seeing effect, and when he spoke there was
nary a quiver in his meticulous beard as he unrolled his restrained
and cumbersome sentences. He lacked any flash of wit or humour
and refused to utter any word of abuse even in the most aggra-
vating of circumstances, usually arranging to leave that dirty little
task to his underlings. On the night of his humiliating defeat as a
member of parliament by Manitoba voters in 1880, for instance,
he remarked to HBC Factor James Cole: "I am sorry to say that

*(Opposite) Sir Donald Smith, as
photographed by Notman in 1895.*

a majority of the intelligent electorate of my late Selkirk constituency have, in the exercise of their undoubted privilege and right to choose the most fit and proper person available for the purpose of representing them in the Dominion Parliament, seen fit to reject my own humble, not hitherto unacceptable person." On cue, Cole recapped succinctly: "The damn voters took your money and voted against you!"

"You," Smith intoned, "have properly expressed the situation."

During the decades before and after the turn of the century, Smith was one of Canada's best-known if not best-loved public figures. Invitations to the many receptions at the largest of his four homes, a baronial red-stone castle at 1157 Dorchester Street in Montreal, were sought by every social climber in the city. Smith was a snob to the point of keeping a secret tally classifying his guests according to rank. The roll call included a future king and queen (George V and Queen Mary, who came to Canada in 1901 as the Duke and Duchess of Cornwall and York), a prince and princess, eight dukes, seven marquises, twenty-one earls, six viscounts, six governors-general, twenty-six lieutenant-governors, seven prime ministers, twenty-seven provincial premiers, four archbishops, seventeen bishops, twenty-nine supreme court judges, fourteen chief justices, thirty-one mayors and fifty-eight generals. Smith's list tidily subdivided this latter category into forty-seven generals of the Imperial Army and eleven colonial troop commanders.

Smith's Dorchester Street mansion in Montreal.

Fitted more by temperament than by birth for the aristocratic life, Smith ruled his household with humourless mastery. Once, while having breakfast with Dr Wilfred Grenfell, he watched the lamp under the hot water kettle falter and die. When the missionary moved to relight it, Smith stopped him and angrily summoned his butler. "Remember, James," he pronounced, "you have only certain duties to perform. This is one. Never, under any circumstances, let such an omission occur again."

Such peremptory arrogance was particularly irksome to those who knew Smith's inauspicious background. He was born on August 6, 1820 (the same year George Simpson was brought into the HBC), at Forres, a storied Scottish town in the middle of that brooding countryside where Shakespeare pictured Macbeth and Banquo meeting the prophetic witches. His adolescence was much less influenced by his father, a tradesman clinging to solvency with alcoholic indecision, than by his uncle, John Stuart. Stuart had been second-in-command during Simon Fraser's exploration of the Fraser River's headwaters in 1808 and later became an HBC Factor at Lesser Slave Lake. Following his unspectacular graduation from the local grammar school, young Donald began to labour as a clerk in the town lawyer's office.

When he was eighteen, his uncle arrived home on furlough and offered to recommend Smith for a junior HBC Clerkship. The youngster accepted eagerly, though his first job was counting muskrat skins in the stuffy Hudson's Bay warehouse at Lachine for "twenty pounds a year and all found." Four years later he was finally promoted to Junior Trader at Tadoussac, an isolated St Lawrence River trading post near the mouth of the Saguenay.

Forced to toil far from a world he had just begun to appreciate, removed from the events in which he wanted to play a part, he began to feel a gnawing need for self-assertion that never left him. The self-created pressures that made him one of the most frigid, class-conscious aristocrats of his era had their roots during those years of lonely treks through the Saguenay forests. When his cabin caught fire during the summer of 1847, Smith fed the flames with his clothes and private papers, cackling incoherently in maddened frustration; that fall, he began to feel the symptoms of increasing snowblindness, but his requests for compassionate leave were repeatedly denied.

When the schooner *Marten* called at Tadoussac on her way to Montreal, he deserted. After Montreal doctors had examined him and declared there was nothing wrong with his eyes, the autocratic George Simpson punished Smith for breaking the rules by assigning him to the Company's version of hell: North West River (now Fort Chimo), a derelict trading post in central Labrador. There Smith learned his harshest lessons in corporate survival. The misery of his posting was relieved only by his marriage to Isabella Hardisty, the daughter of an HBC chief trader. She had come north with her family and had married James Grant, one of Smith's fellow traders, but without benefit of church ritual. A few months later the lady exercised her prerogative to change her mind and picked Smith as her husband – a marriage that was legalized half a century later in a secret ceremony at the British Embassy in Paris.

Smith returned to England for a holiday in 1864 and so impressed Hudson's Bay officials during his London visit that five years later he was transferred out of Labrador to Montreal as the Company's Chief Factor. Second-guessing the effects of the Grand Trunk Railway's progress westward, Smith realized that the HBC Charter would soon have to be abandoned and that the Company's rights had to be renegotiated. Determined to profit by the change, he had speculated in HBC shares and done extremely well (probably with inside information) when the stock was watered by 400 percent in 1863. Smith was appalled by the lack of cost control exercised by the London management and by the treatment of its overseas employees. The Company's factors and traders were due 40 percent of the profits by the old Deed Poll, yet their claims were being ignored, partly because they had no one to represent them. At several meetings at Norway House, Smith whipped the senior employees into a coalition. By threatening to withdraw and start a new Montreal-based North West Company backed by the Bank of Montreal, Smith was able to appropriate for his peers a good chunk of the £300,000 paid to the Company by the Canadian government for property rights to Rupert's Land. In April 1869 the nervous London Committeemen appointed Donald Smith as Chief Commissioner for Montreal and Labrador and, later, of the whole service.

Isabella Smith, Lady Strathcona

The newly installed Dominion government had meanwhile sent surveyors to the Prairies with instructions to parcel the settlers' land into mile-square sections, with little regard for the traditional strip-farming methods of its Métis occupants. The move rallied support for their leader, Louis Riel, who stopped the Ottawa-appointed governor of the region from entering his territory and defiantly captured Fort Garry. In Ottawa, Sir John A. Macdonald recognized that the country did not have transportation facilities adequate for the wintertime dispatch of troops to quell the rebellion by force. Because Hudson's Bay Company interests were so vitally concerned, he appointed Smith to investigate the insurrection.

Making use of the clan connections of his wife Isabella (whose mother was a Scottish Métis and a Sutherland) and of his own mother (who was distantly connected to the family of Cuthbert Grant), Smith travelled about the Red River Settlement during the winter of 1870 recruiting the support of "kinfolk" and religious leaders. He soon pulled together a party of citizens opposed to Riel's putative Métis republic. At a great open-air meeting inside the fort, he dramatically put the case against Riel, effectively turning the tide against those who wanted out-and-out independence or union with the United States. Icicles hung from Smith's beard as he stood beside Riel in a numbing twenty-below wind, promising fair treatement by the Canadian government to the mustered settlers. The meeting elected forty representatives to study the proposals. In an attempt to reassert his authority, Riel later executed Thomas Scott, a particularly quarrelsome Orangeman, setting off the sequence of events that would eventually defeat his cause.

When Smith returned to Ottawa, he recommended that an armed expedition be sent to Fort Garry the following summer to reimpose the rule of law. The troops entered the fort on August

21, 1870, without firing a shot. In his report to Macdonald, Smith had also suggested that a permanent semi-military force be established in the region; this resulted in formation of the North West Mounted Police, predecessors of the Royal Canadian Mounted Police.

Smith capitalized on his popularity with the Fort Garry settlers by winning the Winnipeg seat in the first Manitoba legislature and in 1871 became federal MP for Selkirk. Named the Hudson's Bay Resident Governor that same year, he began to evaluate the potential of the land assets retained by the Company after the sale of the bulk of those assets to the Crown. He foresaw that where buffalo grazed, cattle would one day feed, and that much of the Prairies (which were favoured with two hours more sunshine a day during the maturing season than any other wheat-growing region in the world) could become rich farmland. While other shareholders panicked during the complicated transfer of power, Smith bought up great blocks of Hudson's Bay stock at depressed prices and gradually acquired enough shares to exercise working control of the Company. On some of this stock he eventually realized a 1,300 percent profit. Smith changed the emphasis of the HBC's operations from fur to land. He sold so much of its remaining territory, in fact, that the Hudson's Bay Company later had to repurchase chunks of its former holdings for the construction of department stores at many times the original price.

Louis Riel at the time of the Red River Rebellion in 1869.

Smith's blossoming business reputation prompted many of the Hudson's Bay factors to send him their savings to invest for them. With these funds and his own growing fortune, he captured stock control of the Bank of Montreal and used that fiscal base to become one of the chief animating partners in the financing of the Canadian Pacific Railway. He quickly became the wealthiest Canadian of his day.

Cautiously investing the HBC's land profits in rudimentary shops to serve the new Prairie settlers, he borrowed members of Harrods management from London in an attempt to make his emporia into miniatures of the doughty British department store.

A year after the CPR line was completed in 1886, Smith was knighted. Fearing that he might swing behind Liberal leader Sir Wilfrid Laurier, the Tories appointed the seventy-six-year-old financier-politician Canadian High Commissioner to the United Kingdom in 1896. London society immediately adopted the former Labrador fur-trader as its favourite colonial character. Queen Victoria called him "His Labrador Lordship," or, in more familiar moments, "Uncle Donald." "You talk with him," wrote A.G. Gardiner, editor of the London *Daily News*, "and it is as if Canada

YUKON GOLD

In 1896 gold was discovered at Bonanza Creek, just off the Klondike River in the Yukon Territory. By the fall of 1897, word was out and the stampede to the gold fields was on. The North West Mounted Police, in an attempt to make sure would-be prospectors didn't enter the territory unequipped, patrolled the passes into the Yukon, turning back those without proper supplies.

Always ready to take advantage of an opportunity, the Hudson's Bay Company quickly jumped into the sourdough supply business. For those going to the Klondike (or "Klondyke" as the Company's brochure called it), a complete miner's outfit could be purchased at any of the Bay's western stores. The outfit included everything from flour to wool underwear to gold pans.

Edmonton was one of the major staging points for those heading north to seek their fortunes, and the Hudson's Bay Store there seems to have been especially eager for their business. In a large exterior sign, it promised "Complete outfits supplied on shortest notice." Since the overland trail from Edmonton proved to be one of the slowest routes to the gold fields, it's unlikely that the Bay's speedy outfitting gave anyone a head start.

(Right) A Hudson's Bay Company flyer advertising supplies for gold miners. For between $190 and $220, a miner could buy the supplies he required for one year in the gold country.
(Opposite, top) The Hudson's Bay Company store at Edmonton in 1898. For those entering the Klondike overland from Canada, Edmonton was the last supply stop on the way.
(Opposite, bottom) Newly outfitted goldseekers head off from the Hudson's Bay store in Edmonton.

GOODS PURCHASED IN CANADA DO NOT HAVE TO BEAR DUTIES AS THE MINES ARE IN CANADIAN TERRITORY

FOR ALL INFORMATION WRITE TO THE HUDSON'S BAY COMPANY AT WINNIPEG. VICTORIA. CALGARY. VANCOUVER. EDMONTON.

KLONDYKE GOLD FIELDS
HUDSON'S BAY COMPANY
FULLY EQUIPPED STORES
MINERS & PROSPECTORS

A MINER'S OUTFIT.

ESTIMATED REQUIREMENTS FOR ONE MAN FOR ONE YEAR.

PROVISIONS.

Apples, evaporated	20 lbs.
Apricots. "	15 "
Bacon	200 "
Baking powder	10 "
Barley, pot	10 "
Beans	100 "
Beef extract	1 doz.
Candles	25 lbs.
Coffee	10 "
Corn Meal	20 ".
Flour	500 "
Lime juice	1 gal.
Matches	5 boxes
Milk, condensed	1 doz.
Mustard	1 lb.
Oats, rolled	50 "
Peas, split	10 "
Pepper	1 "
Prunes	10 "
Rice	25 "
Salt	20 "
Soap	10 "
Soda, baking	2 "
Sugar	75 "
Tea, compressed	10 "
Tobacco, smoking	10 "
Vegetables, compressed	12 "
Yeast Cakes	8 doz.

CLOTHING.

Blankets	2 pairs
Cap, cloth	1 only
Cap, fur	1 "
Coats, corduroy lined or buckskin	1 "
" Oilskin	1 "
Dunnage Bag	1 "
Gloves, skin	1 pair
" wool	1 "
Goggles, snow	1 only
Handkerchiefs, colored	1 doz.
Mitts, leather	1 pair
Mitts, wool	2 "
Mosquito netting	10 yds.
Overalls	2 pairs
Pants, moleskin	1 "
Sheet, ground	1 only
Shirts, flannel	8 only
" mackinaw	1 "
Socks, wool	12 pairs
Suspenders	1 pair
Sweaters, wool	2 only
Towels	1 doz.
Underwear, wool	8 suits

FOOTWEAR.

Boots, laced	2 pair
Boots, rubber	1 "
Duffles	2 "
Moccasins,	8 "
Socks, long Arctic	2 "
Snow shoes	1 "

HARDWARE.

Auger	1 only
Axe, chopping	1 "
Brace and bits	1 set
Camp kettles	1 nest
Chisel	1 only
Coffee pot	1 "
Compass, pocket	1 "
Cup, tin	1 "
Knife, butcher's	1 "
Knife and fork	1 "
Files	8 "
Fry pan	1 "
Gold pan	1 "
Hammer	1 "
Hatchet	1 "
Nails, assorted	20 lbs.
Oakum	10 "
Picks, miner's	2 only
Pick handles	8 "
Pitch	10 lbs.
Plates, tin	2 only
Rope	25 lbs.
Saw, hand	1 only
" whip	1 "
Saw set	1 "
Scales, gold	1 set
Screw driver	1 only
Shovels, miner's	2 "
Spoons, assorted	8 "

Approximate cost of above outfit (subject to market fluctuations) will be:

at WINNIPEG CALGARY EDMONTON VANCOUVER and VICTORIA	From $190 to $220, according to the point at which purchased.

FOR PARTIES, the cost per man can be diminished according to numbers, as several of the articles can be used in common.

TENTS AND ANY OTHER REQUIREMENTS can be supplied according to the season for travelling and route selected.

H.B.Co OLD STORE
EDMONTON 1897.

COPYRIGHT
ERNEST BROWN

OUTFITTING
FOR KLONDYKE
AT H.B.Co's STORE
EDMONTON 1898

Donald Smith driving the last spike in the building of the Canadian Pacific Railway on November 7, 1885.

(Opposite) This beautifully illustrated letter sent to the Bay in 1920 by Charles M. Russell, the famed American frontier painter, expresses the difference between the new Bay and the old: "Forty years ago when I came to Montana thair were a few forts in Alberta but no towns...thair were no lady clerks with the Hudson Bay but men who knew nothing of lace or lingerie but could tell a cow robe from a bull with thair eyes shut.... That life has gone and most of the men who lived it but the Hudson Bay still lives in its big stores...."

stands before you, telling her astonishing story." Elevated to the peerage in 1897, he chose as his official crest a beaver gnawing a maple tree. As "Baron Strathcona and Mount Royal, of Glencoe, in the County of Argyll, and of Mount Royal, in the Province of Quebec and Dominion of Canada," he represented Canada in London for the next eighteen years.

When Lord Strathcona died of heart failure at ninety-three on January 21, 1914, he had outlived most of the violent animosities he had created as plain Donald Alexander Smith. By then he had gained a reputation as one of the English-speaking world's great philanthropists. He gave away $12 million during his lifetime, and another $20 million in his will. His most dramatic gift, and probably the most deliberately spectacular action in his life, was his donation in 1900 of a fully-equipped mounted regiment to help the British fight the South African War. Smith had analyzed reports of the Boer successes against the sedulously drilled British infantry and knew they needed a mobile troop of mounted scouts. He offered a million dollars to raise the Lord Strathcona's Horse – an army of six hundred North West Mounted Police veterans. Volunteers included a hundred adventurous Arizona cowboys who offered to enlist their own horses, but Smith turned them down.

In late 1900, as the troops travelled by train toward their embarkation headquarters in Halifax, well-wishers thronged them at every stop. The citizens of Sudbury presented Colonel Sam Steele, their commanding officer, with a battle flag on which was stitched the simple but earnest tribute: "We are proud of the Empire. We are proud of our Queen. We are proud of Lord

Sept 5th
1920

Mr Charles H Fair Dear Sir
I am slow thanking you for the Hudson Bay Co
history you kindly sent me
I like History and that old fur compeney has made lots of it
Thair is hardly a City ore town in your Country that did
not spring from a Hudson Bay stockade. They were
trail brakers of Canada
forty years ago when I came to Montana thair were a
few Forts in Alberta but no towns
long ago when the Black feet came with robe and sent
thair nacked pipe carrier thair were no lady crarks
with the Hudson Bay But men who new nothing of lace
ore lingerie but could tell a cow robe from a bull
with thair eyes shut they savyed a gun and thair
hands were never fare from one when they traded over
the log counter with a black foot
That life has gon and most of the men who lived it
but the Hudson Bay still lives in its big stores
Thanking you again for the History
Sincerly yours C M Russell

Strathcona." The regiment fought in South Africa for a year with considerable success.

Charitable Strathcona may have been, but his snobbery extended beyond the grave. Though his will directed that money be set aside for the establishment of a leper colony, it had a strict entrance requirement – only leprous English gentlemen of good standing could be admitted.

Strathcona was eventually succeeded as HBC Governor by Sir Robert Kindersley (of the Bank of England), who during World War I undertook, for a one percent fee, to supply France and later Russia with food and munitions. Through an elaborate maze of subsidiaries and overseas agencies, the Hudson's Bay Company (with a fleet of nearly three hundred merchant ships under charter) became a massive mover of edibles, fuel, lumber, ammunition and troops. More than thirteen million tons of supplies were delivered to France alone. By the spring of 1918, the Company's impressive armada was discharging eleven thousand tons of freight daily at French ports; about a hundred vessels flying the Company's flag had been sunk. The HBC later applied its northern shipping experience to delivering similar cargoes to Czarist Russia and took charge of supplying the White Russian armies following the Bolshevik Revolution. It was on the Archangel run in 1917 that the HBC supply ship *Nascopie* sank a German submarine with its deck gun.

After the demobilization of 1918, the HBC was able to sell four hundred thousand acres of Prairie land at $15 an acre. But peace brought a renewal of competition in the fur trade as Lamson & Hubbard of Boston purchased its competing Diamond P stores in the Peace River and built steamboats to ply the Mackenzie River Valley. Looking for new markets, the Company accelerated its move into the Arctic, purchasing Captain Scott's old exploration ship the *Discovery* and a series of small toughly built freighters that were to supply the posts of Labrador and Hudson Bay for the next seventy years.

During the 1920s, the HBC's traders moved by swift dogsled and flimsy ski-plane into the Eskimo lands of the great northern archipelago, pursuing glossy sealskin and silver fox furs for the elegant salons of Mayfair, Rue de Rivoli and Fifth Avenue. In this one decade, Fur Trade Commissioner Ralph Parsons, "the King of Baffin Land," opened fifteen new northern posts.

Charles Townshend, who had worked for Unilever's marketing department, was brought in by Governor C.V. Sale (who succeeded Kindersley) to exploit Eskimo craftsmanship and the whale oil resources of the Arctic. After several years of joint ventures

(continued on page 194)

SHIPS OF THE BAY

The Hudson's Bay Company was a land empire, but from its earliest days, its trade depended on ships. The first posts established in the Fur Country were far to the north of any existing European settlements. To keep these posts supplied with trade goods, and to bring back the harvest of furs, supply ships made their way to and from the old world annually. These ships (there were usually three of them) ran from Gravesend on the Thames, via the Orkneys, to the Company's posts on the Bay. This was a pattern the Company was to keep up for more than two centuries, until transportation improved between Canada's North and southern centres.

Other ships played important roles in the Company's history. One of the most famous was, appropriately enough, named the *Beaver*. The first steamship ever to fly the Hudson's Bay Company flag, she entered service with the HBC in 1835 and was employed on Canada's west coast. Capable of entering narrow fiords and inlets, her function was as much public relations as trade. George Simpson reasoned that a steam-powered ship would have the effect of "overawing the natives."

In the twentieth century, the Company's fleet continued to play a varied and important role. Ocean-going ships ferried supplies to the New World, tough little freighters pushed their way through the ice of Hudson Bay and sternwheelers moved goods along the Mackenzie and other rivers.

(Below) This work by an unknown nineteenth-century artist shows the Company barque Prince Rupert *under sail. The HBC crest can be clearly seen on the flag atop her main mast.*
(Overleaf) Ships could serve as mobile trading posts. In this painting by the Arctic explorer Robert Hood, the HBC ships Prince of Wales *and* Eddystone *are engaged in bartering with the Eskimos.*

THE BEAVER

Built to trade along Canada's Pacific coast, the *Beaver* was a difficult ship to keep going. She required a crew of thirteen cutters to cut wood for her and four stokers to feed her boilers. After thirty-one years of service to the Company, and an additional twenty-one years of surveying and log-towing, she ran aground in 1888, and her skeletal hulk (right) was left to rot.

THE DISCOVERY

Originally the flagship of the polar explorer Captain Scott, the Hudson's Bay Company purchased this durable whaler in 1905, the year after she returned from Antarctica. Now a historic monument moored in the Thames, her eighteen years of service with the Company were spent in the bay trade.

THE NASCOPIE

A stout little steamer, the *Nascopie* was a fixture in Hudson Bay for many years. In the First World War, she gained a measure of fame by sinking a German U-Boat while ferrying suplies to Russia. Shown here as she appeared in 1934, the *Nascopie* sank off Cape Dorset in 1947 after hitting an uncharted reef.

FORT McMURRAY

The *Fort McMurray* was a typical example of the sternwheelers the Company used to move people and supplies along the rivers of the Canadian north. Of very shallow draft, they could land almost anywhere and if they ran aground could often be backed up.

THE BAY GOES TO HOLLYWOOD

The story of the Hudson's Bay Company was a natural for Hollywood—a saga that involved kings, lords and trappers and unfolded amidst the very scenery where Nelson Eddy wooed Jeanette Macdonald. But ever conscious of its image, the Company had blocked previous efforts to bring its name to the screen. To 20th Century-Fox's *Hudson's Bay*, however, official sanction was given. Paul Muni starred as Radisson, Vincent Price put in a cameo as Charles II, and Gene Tierney played the love interest.

When *Hudson's Bay* premiered in January 1941, the Bay department stores promoted it enthusiastically. Thanks in part to these efforts, the film was a commercial success, especially in Western Canada. Critics complained that the film lacked much in the way of action and today this classic shows up only on late-night television, if at all.

Gene Tierney poses with a Hudson's Bay blanket, a gift from the Company.
(Right) Paul Muni as Radisson stands second from the left while Groseilliers kneels below.

192

PAUL MUNI in
HUDSON'S BAY
with GENE **TIERNEY** LAIRD **CREGAR** JOHN **SUTTON**
VIRGINIA **FIELD** VINCENT **PRICE** NIGEL **BRUCE**
DIRECTED BY IRVING PICHEL · ASSOCIATE PRODUCER KENNETH MACGOWAN
A 20TH CENTURY-FOX PICTURE

(Left) As the fictional Lady Barbara, Gene Tierney gave the film some female allure.

(Top) The three male stars ham it up with Eskimo pies. (Middle) Portaging on a soundstage. (Bottom) Store displays promoted both the movie and Hudson's Bay blankets.

193

In the period between the wars, bush planes were used increasingly to supply small, isolated posts.

with Imperial Oil, the Bay signed a partnership with the flamboyant E.W. Marland (backed by J.P. Morgan) and founded Hudson's Bay Oil & Gas to develop the potential of its retained mineral rights. With the rapid depletion of the beaver, conservation reserves were established, and fur farms run by independents soon began to provide a larger portion of the supply. HBC fur profits increasingly came from "middleman" activities such as auctioneering and warehousing.

In the aftermath of the 1929 stockmarket crash, the HBC experienced a shareholders' revolt when a group of unhappy investors alleged that Governor Sale and others had misappropriated funds by hiding them in a subsidiary that paid no dividends to the HBC. Sale resigned, and was replaced after an interregnum by a tough, elegant Aberdonian financier, Patrick Ashley Cooper of the Bank of England. He was a well-known specialist in broken-down companies, whose most recent patient, the government of Great Britain, he had pronounced a hopeless case. A smart City accountant and fix-it man, born in middle circumstances in Aberdeen but with a Cambridge oar and friends in high places, Patrick Ashley Cooper was the favourite choice of "Mad Montague" Norman, Governor of the Bank of England, to take over the ailing HBC. Flattened by the Depression and anemic after twenty-five years of asset-stripping and overspending, the Company had unloaded most of its prime Western land and leased away its treasure chest of mineral rights.

Cooper was a new type of financier, a fussy bureaucrat in a bowler hat who came to love the Company so much that he had to

To encourage their customers to get out and trap, HBC posts were frequently unheated.

be shoved into retirement and negotiated out of its Governorship. A tall, awkward Scot with round black tortoiseshell glasses and a crisp military moustache, Cooper was a bit too "old school tie" for many of the Canadians in the HBC, but he was kindlier and more approachable than Kindersley or Sale had ever been. He ran the firm much like the headmaster of a boys' school. After three years of severe losses and the dropping of share values to £1, Cooper visited Canada and recommended closing scores of posts and sales shops, a tactic that resulted in great hardship and some starvation in the North. Throughout the 1930s, Cooper pared operating expenses to the bone while still finding the cash to buy out such competitors as Revillon Frères, Lamson & Hubbard and the Canalaska Trading Company of the Western Arctic, giving the HBC a virtual monopoly over northern trade.

Cooper moved the day-to-day management of the Company to Canada under a British accountant named Philip Chester. The two, fuddy-duddies both, battled each other for most of two decades like well-bred scorpions in a bottle. But after three years with average losses of $1.5 million, they turned the Company around, making a modest $150,000 profit in 1933. During the late 1940s Cooper presided over the most glorious London Board since the Company's birth. Directors included Field Marshal Viscount Alanbrooke, the wizard of mechanized warfare; Sir Edward Peacock, the tough and well-connected Canadian-born financier and former Upper Canada College housemaster who later headed Barings, London's oldest merchant bank, which was so influential its officers in effect ran the Bank of England and acted as financial advisor to the Royal family; Sir William ("Tony") Keswick, scion of the old opium-smuggling firm of Jardine Matheson, the "Taipans" of Hong Kong and "Ichibans" of the Japan trade (Lord Montgomery's chief finance officer before Normandy, Keswick eventually succeeded Cooper as Governor); and the glamorous Victor Cazalet, president of the Eton Society and four-time British (and once Canadian) squash champion.

During the years following the Second World War, chinchilla ranching and mink mutations drastically reduced the demand for wild fur. Under the firm hand of Governor Tony Keswick, Hudson's Bay Oil & Gas came back to life with more than $300 million invested in exploration during the next two decades. Inspired by the House of Fraser's takeover of Harrods, the Bay bought Montreal's venerable ten-store Morgan's chain in 1960 and with that acquisition finally became a national retailer.

By the late 1960s, punitive British tax laws and withdrawal of the old and advantageous "Overseas Trading Companies Concessions" made moving the HBC's headquarters to Canada imperative to its survival. With its capable yet diplomatic Canadian Managing Director, Richard Murray, leading the way, the transfer was orderly and relatively tranquil. The Royal Charter was revised and Elizabeth II, as Queen of Canada, duly proclaimed the new version. In 1970, shortly before the signing of the Treaty of Brussels admitting the United Kingdom to the European Community, the HBC became a Canadian company with head office in Winnipeg.

After putting down corporate roots in Canada, a decade of rampaging growth saw the HBC expand into a corporate behemoth, establishing Eaton-Bay Financial Services, a cooperative trust with one of its rivals, and taking over many ventures, including the Freiman's chain in Ottawa, Calgary's Siebens Oil & Gas and Roxy Petroleum, Markborough Properties, and the Zellers and Simpsons department store chains. The Hudson's Bay Company was now Canada's pre-eminent retailer (with more than six hundred stores) a major player in Canadian shopping-mall developments and a retail colossus with annual sales of more than $5 billion.

While the Hudson's Bay Company was occupied with its corporate hopscotch to Canada, a middle-aged Canadian who was a believer in the romantic and entrepreneurial spirit of the British Empire was making heavy investments in the United Kingdom. Roy Thomson was born in Toronto, the son of a Cabbagetown barber. After failing in the auto parts business and peddling obsolete crystal radio sets in Northern Ontario, he got into publishing in North Bay and by 1953 had amassed a medium-sized Canadian newspaper empire. A tough bird with Coke-bottle-bottom spectacles, usually attired in floppy suits draped over his bulky frame, Thomson decided at 59 that his line of credit would allow him to speculate in more exotic fields. After a careful search of U.K. balance sheets, he bought the *Scotsman* of Edinburgh and shortly afterwards won the franchise for Scottish Television, which he described to a delighted press as "a licence to print money." In a classically elegant reverse takeover engineered by the Warburgs, Thomson then took control of the *Sunday Times* and *Times* of London. Before the family dumped the featherbedded newspapers fifteen years later, they had lost £70 million, but his rescue of the Fleet Street "Thunderer" earned Roy Thomson his cherished peerage.

Scottish connections led J. Paul Getty and Armand Hammer to approach Thomson and offer him 20 percent of the Occidental consortium preparing to drill in the North Sea, where oil had been discovered by Phillips in 1969. Roy Thomson pledged his entire family holdings and joined the consortium; oil was going for $3.60 a barrel. Occidental struck it rich in the Piper Field on the third try. Thomson rolled the dice once more, and in 1974 Occidental struck oil in the Claymore field. In 1976 Piper began producing — at $14 a barrel —moving the Thomson holdings into the billion-dollar range.

Kenneth Thomson stands in front of some of the paintings in his extensive art collection.

As Roy Thomson passed from the scene, his son Ken inherited a well-greased money machine. Piper was producing two hundred and fifty thousand barrels a day, fifty thousand of which were his. By 1978 the family companies were debt-free and grossing at least $300 million a year in oil revenues. Not the kind of sum you keep in a savings account. The Hudson's Bay Company seemed the perfect takeover target. Its historic pedigree suited a British-Canadian lord, and Simpsons, which the Company had just acquired, was expected to turn around soon, promising impressive bottom-line results. In 1979, Ken Thomson purchased, for $640 million cash, 17 1/2 million shares of the Hudson's Bay Company, or 76 percent of the total — a larger stake than any individual had ever held before.

Whatever its future promise, the company Thomson took over was far from healthy. The early-eighties recession, the debt accumulated during the 1978 and 1979 takeover binges (totalling $2 billion by 1982), and rising interest rates all played a part. In 1984, the Hudson's Bay Company lost $107 million. By 1987, losses were mounting to $300 million. Thomson — with the aid of his astute corporate strategist, Toronto lawyer John Tory — set about to achieve what Simpson and Smith had done before him: give the world's oldest capitalist company a new lease on life.

Central to this was a "disposal plan" for thirteen non-core businesses. Among these were the HBC's 178 northern stores and its fur auction houses as well — what many regarded as the Company's very soul. These were harsh moves, but they were necessary to reduce the Company's debt and, as Lord Thomson explained it, to concentrate management and financial resources where they were needed most, on the Company's core businesses of department-store retailing and real estate. Nevertheless, the decision saddened and angered loyal Company veterans, who were only partially mollified when the enterprising new owners of the northern stores revived the name and insignia of the Company's long-dormant enemy, the North West Company.

If he were at all disposed towards nostalgia, George Kosich might have laid personal claim to the Nor'Wester's old motto, "PERSEVERANCE!" In Kosich, Thomson found the ultimate weapon to guarantee the Company's survival. An adept retailer with twenty-seven years at the Bay, Kosich was appointed HBC president and chief operating officer in 1987. Tough and single-minded, he had already spent two years as executive vice-president responsible for HBC's department stores, including Simpsons. For a key meeting in Vancouver, dubbed the "seagull summit," Kosich pulled together people from different areas of the Company — from the Bay and Simpsons, from sales promotion, merchandising and regional offices — and set to work taking apart the Company. Says Kosich: "We had to downsize, we had to rationalize, we had to consolidate, we had to restructure." His proclivity for closing unprofitable units and cutting expenses earned him the nickname George Carnage, but Kosich knew that cutting was not enough. Equal attention was given to boosting sales.

The Bay became what is called a "category killer" in profitable areas such as women and men's apparel, cosmetics and small housewares such as china, by offering the broadest assortment in all price ranges for those commodities. To control costs, the Company began bypassing suppliers and buying much of its own merchandise, in the process rediscovering its roots as an overseas trading company by purchasing Linmark, a major buying organization in the Far East. Downtown flagship stores were restored to their former glory. In 1993, the Company acquired the Woodward's chain, gaining twenty-one new Bay and Zellers stores, among them coveted locations in Calgary and Vancouver. The only division that never stopped bleeding was the Toronto-centric Simpsons. Management tried everything — moving the stores upscale, taking them back downscale, adding the country's most expensive food hall — but none of it worked. In 1991, with the economy mired in a recession and the Company tired of throwing money and effort at it, the division closed down. Kosich says today that, given the chance to do it over again, he would have been much quicker to shut down Simpsons.

At Zellers, the discount-store chain acquired in 1978, Kosich's

The Hudson's Bay Company purchased the Vancouver-based Woodward's chain in 1993 and converted its stores to Bay and Zellers outlets.

new regimen resulted in almost immediate success. Zellers had been spending a lot of money to upgrade the stores' physical appearance in the hope of becoming an "upscale discounter" — a retailing oxymoron. Under Kosich, those plans were scrapped, to be replaced by the lowest operating costs in the industry. Zellers' new slogan was "The lowest price is the law." Lower costs meant lower prices, and that drove up sales. In the first four years of Kosich's presidency, Zellers profits tripled, and Zellers remains the top profit producer among discount retailers. Intensified competition, resulting from the 1994 incursion by U.S. giant Wal-Mart, was greeted by an aggressive counterattack. For all the changes it has undergone in recent years, this remains the same Company that has, over a span of 325 years, successfully fended off similar raids by foreign powers. In their time, d'Iberville's French fleet and the armies of voyageurs sent out by the North West Company must have seemed just as menacing.

Markborough Properties — one of the country's largest real estate firms — was spun off to HBC shareholders in 1990, and for the first time since 1870 the HBC was now mainly in one line of business — retailing. In 1992 the Thomsons sold 20 million shares to a group of underwriters for $545 million, reducing their stake to 23 percent, leading some retail analysts to speculate it could lead to foreign control of the HBC. Thomson and Tory left the Company a retailing giant with record earnings in 1993, but one without a majority shareholder, and facing an ever-unpredictable future.

Even with its ancient Charter and royal land grant, however, there has rarely been anything resembling certainty in the history of the Hudson's Bay Company. For the pioneering clerks who sat out their lives in the bleak forts around Hudson Bay, even bare survival was not guaranteed. They were ordinary men, by and large, castaways in a tight-fisted land, yet they achieved something truly magnificent. They endured. The retailing environment at the end of the twentieth century is no more certain, yet more than merely enduring, the Company prospers.

Perhaps the secret of this ultimate example of social Darwinism is that the kings, dukes, knights, accountants and retailers who spent three and a quarter centuries guiding the destiny of the Company of Adventurers have always applied the philosophy contained in the stern dictum by British Prime Minister Lord Palmerston in 1848: "We have no eternal allies and we have no perpetual enemies. Our interests are eternal and perpetual."

Appointed president of the Hudson's Bay Company in 1987, George Kosich turned the company around by cutting costs and boosting sales.

199

THE RETAIL EMPIRE

By 1870, the fur trade was finished as a major industry. But the Hudson's Bay Company had already moved into land sales and later into merchandising and retailing — feeding and supplying the farmers to whom it had sold off its huge tracts of real estate. With the opening of the first really urban Hudson's Bay Company store in Vancouver in 1887, the modern-day retail empire was born. By the 1930s, Hudson's Bay stores dominated important corners in the downtowns of Calgary, Vancouver, Edmonton and Winnipeg, home of the Company's flagship store.

The Company remained essentially western-based until 1960 when it purchased the Montreal-based Morgan's chain. Later, under its new, shorter name, "The Bay," it expanded rapidly throughout eastern Canada. By 1978, thanks to its purchase of the Zellers and Simpsons chains, the Hudson's Bay Company became the largest retailer in Canada.

(Opposite) Behind a reconstruction of old Fort Edmonton stands the modern city that grew from a Hudson's Bay Company fort. HBC trading posts like the one at Pincher Creek (below) were eventually to evolve into more sophisticated outlets like the Bay stores of today (right).

(Below) Edmonton's Jasper Avenue in the 1880s featured a Bay store, as does (left) Toronto's busy Bloor and Yonge intersection today.

(Above left, top and bottom) These displays highlight both the Bay's present strengths in women's fashions (top) and the company's traditional products, such as the classic Hudson's

Bay blanket (bottom). (Above) Bay president Bob Peter starred in a series of highly successful commercials, including one featuring Cher.

THE WORLD
OF ZELLERS

Purchased by the Hudson's Bay
Company in 1978, Zellers was founded
as a discount chain by Walter P. Zeller in
1931. The company expanded rapidly in
the 1950s, moving into "park and shop"
developments (as the first malls were
called) hot on the heels of the early
suburbs, and by the early 1960s Zellers
had more than one hundred stores. In
the late 1980s, following the HBC's
takeover and after a brief stab at moving
upscale, Zellers adopted the motto "The
lowest price is the law," and created the
Club Z program to encourage repeat
business. Explosive growth followed, and
by 1993, Zellers' 285 stores had annual
revenues of more than $3 billion.

(Opposite, top) A modern-day Zellers contrasts with (opposite, middle) this line drawing of the company's Winnipeg, Manitoba, location from the 1950s.

(Left) Zellers president Paul Walters, centre, and two employees at an Ontario Store.

(Right) Fashion drawings from Zellers advertising of the 1950s.

(Below) In keeping with the emphasis on constantly increasing sales, Zellers has been building larger and larger stores, such as this one in St. Bruno, Quebec.

(Previous page) A trio of HBC canoes manned by voyageurs disappears into the mist in Frances Ann Hopkins' evocative painting. The artist herself appears in the rear canoe, sitting next to her husband, who was Sir George Simpson's private secretary. The daughter of Admiral Beechey, the Arctic explorer for whom Beechey Island is named, this gentle Englishwoman moved to Montreal in 1858. During the 1860s and '70s she and her husband travelled by canoe with the Governor on his visits to HBC posts. Hopkins recorded the life she saw in her sketchbook and later turned it into large, lush canvases. She again appears with her husband in Canoe Manned by Voyageurs, which is featured on our cover. Other Hopkins paintings can be seen on pages 6–7, 110–111, 114–115 and 224.

(Opposite) Crest from the cover of the Albany Fort account book, 1791–1792.

APPENDICES

CHRONOLOGY

1610
Henry Hudson enters the strait and the bay which now bear his name and trades for furs with one Indian on the shores of James Bay.

1611
Henry Hudson's crew mutiny aboard the *Discovery* and set him and several others adrift in Hudson Bay in a sailing dinghy; their fate is unknown.

1612–1632
Exploration of Hudson Bay by Thomas Button (1612–1632), William Baffin (1615), Jens Munk (1619–20), Luke Foxe (1631–32) and Thomas James (1631–32) shows it to be landlocked.

1636
Sixteen-year-old Rupert and his brother Carl Louis arrive in London in February, exiles from Bohemia.

1649
Charles I is tried and beheaded. His son is proclaimed Charles II, but goes into exile with his court. Rupert becomes a privateer to bolster the family's finances.

1651
Pierre Radisson settles in Trois Rivières.

1654–56
Médard Chouart, Sieur Des Groseilliers, is trading among the "Far Indians."

1659
Radisson and Groseilliers embark in August on a private trading expedition west of Lake Superior to the upper Missouri and Mississippi.

1660
Radisson and Groseilliers travel among the tribes of the Great Lakes, returning to Montreal on August 20 with a rich load of furs; they propose exporting pelts via Hudson Bay but are arrested and fined because their journey had been "unauthorized." With Charles II's coronation on May 8, the Stuarts are restored to the English throne. Pepys begins his diary.

1662
Rupert returns to settle in London, involved with the newly chartered "Royal Adventurers trading into Africa." The Royal Society is incorporated. Radisson and Groseilliers announce their departure for Hudson Bay from Quebec but sail to New England instead.

1665
Bubonic plague sweeps London (one hundred thousand out of a population of six hundred thousand succumb, and many flee). Radisson and Groseilliers meet Colonel George Cartwright in Boston, are in London by late in the year, and Oxford shortly afterwards.

1666
Radisson and Groseilliers meet Charles II, then stay at Rupert's Windsor Castle apartments until April; French spies try to lure Groseilliers to the Netherlands. On September 2, the commercial City of London is swept by fire.

1667
The Hudson Bay adventurers are organizing their first test voyage, but the war with the Dutch prevents any trip to Hudson Bay. Sir George Carteret buys £20 worth of stock in the new venture on December 20, becoming the first recorded investor.

1668
A preliminary trade syndicate is formed; Radisson, on the *Eaglet*, is forced back to Plymouth on August 5; the *Nonsuch* reaches Hudson Bay; on the east coast of James Bay, the *Nonsuch* crew builds the first fort in the region; while Capt. Zachariah Gillam and Groseilliers trade for pelts, Radisson spends the winter in England writing his travel accounts.

1669
On June 14, the *Nonsuch* leaves Rupert River for England with £1,380 worth of furs, which induces Charles II to prepare a royal charter for the founding of the Company of Adventurers.

1670
The Charter of the Governor and Company of Adventurers is signed by Charles II on May 2, with Prince Rupert as first Governor, a post he holds until his death in 1682.

1671
The *Wivenhoe* and the *Prince Rupert* return from Hudson Bay to London with holds full of furs, thus confirming the feasibility of the new trade venture.

1672
Twenty-seven lots of furs are offered in the company's first public sale, at Garraway's Coffee House on January 24. Moose Factory is established by Radisson and Groseilliers for the HBC.

1673
King Charles presents Radisson with a gold chain and medal on his return to England.

— 1674 —
The Jesuit priest Father Albanel persuades Radisson and Groseilliers to work for France.

— 1676 —
The HBC exports British goods worth £650 and returns a profit of £19,000.

— 1679 —
John Nixon replaces Charles Bayley as Governor at the bay.

— 1681 —
Rupert negotiates customs privileges for the HBC similar to those enjoyed by the Royal African Co. Radisson goes to Canada under instruction from the French government.

— 1682 —
Prince Rupert dies on November 29 at sixty-two of pleurisy and is succeeded the next year as Governor by James, Duke of York (later King James II). The HBC, with five forts on the bay, loses four to the French, retaining only Fort Albany.

— 1684 —
Radisson deserts from the Compagnie du Nord and travels to London to rejoin the HBC for £50 per year and £200 worth of stock.

— 1685 —
John, Lord Churchill (Duke of Marlborough), is appointed HBC Governor.

— 1686 —
The main struggle for possession of the tiny forts on Hudson Bay begins with the expedition of Chevalier de Troyes from Montreal.

— 1687 —
Marlborough petitions James II to argue that the HBC had spent £200,000 on forts and factories destroyed by the French and should be compensated.

— 1690 —
Henry Kelsey begins a series of explorations for the company to the prairie lands, penetrating the interior to south-eastern Saskatchewan. HBC stock trebles in value (a 200 percent stock bonus) to reflect the value of fortifications and establishments; the "Great Dividend" of 74 percent (actually a 25 percent dividend based

on increased stock of £31,500) is declared and paid; HBC is called the only flourishing company in the kingdom, but no dividends are paid out again until 1718. With little opposition Parliament passes a private bill confirming the HBC's monopoly for another seven years.

— 1692 —
The goldsmith-banker Sir Stephen Evans replaces Marlborough as HBC Governor.

— 1694 —
Governor Sir Stephen Evans is ejected from the Customs Board for poor attendance. Radisson sues the HBC for back pay by filing a suit in Chancery Court.

— 1696 —
The English, with four ships, recover all the James Bay forts, and the men of the captured garrisons are taken prisoner to England; Pierre Radisson dies.

— 1697 —
On September 5, Pierre Le Moyne d'Iberville on the *Pélican*, off the mouth of the Nelson River, inflicts defeat on the HBC ships *Hudson's Bay*, *Hampshire* and *Dering*; Fort Nelson is burned; the Treaty of Ryswick, signed in September, leaves the French in possession of all the settlements along the bay (except Fort Albany) for seventeen years. Thomas Lake buys his first HBC stock on May 13 during a drop in the market and becomes a dominant shareholder.

— 1700 —
Sir William Trumbull retires as Governor of the HBC after four years and Sir Stephen Evans takes the post for the second time. Radisson's application for the job of warehouse-keeper is not accepted by the Company.

— 1710 —
Radisson dies in England; his widow Elizabeth (his third wife) is given £6 by the Company for his funeral expenses.

— 1712 —
Sir Bibye Lake is appointed HBC Governor.

— 1713 —
By the signing of the Treaty of Utrecht, France relinquishes all claims to Hudson Bay, which again becomes a British possession.

— 1714 —
James Knight reclaims York Factory. William Stuart explores north of York Factory this summer and next.

— 1719 —
James Knight leads a seaborne expedition for copper and gold north from York Factory.

— 1730 —
HBC critic Arthur Dobbs begins a twenty-year attack on the HBC, accusing the company of failing to explore its granted territories and of reaping great profits.

— 1734 —
Construction on Fort Prince of Wales begins at the mouth of the Churchill River.

— 1743 —
Benjamin Pitt is appointed HBC Governor. Joseph Isbister opens Henley House at the junction of the Albany and Kenogami rivers.

— 1745 —
Bonnie Prince Charlie leads the Jacobite uprising in Scotland; in its aftermath, the British begin to dismantle the clan system. The British Parliament offers a reward of £20,000 for discovery of a North West Passage, and adds an award of £5,000 for reaching the North Pole.

— 1749 —
British House of Commons committee is appointed to consider the trade and territory of the HBC; report favours the HBC and disallows Dobbs' petition.

— 1750 —
Sir Atwell Lake is appointed HBC Governor.

— 1752 —
The HBC London Committee approves a proposal by James Isham, Factor at York, to move inland from the bay to counter French competition.

— 1754 —
Anthony Henday, starting from York Factory, traces the Saskatchewan River inland and becomes the first

white man to see the Rockies, but the Company makes no move to consolidate his findings for half a century.

——————— 1756 ———————

The Seven Years' War begins.

——————— 1761 ———————

The HBC dispatches Captain William Christopher to examine Chesterfield Inlet. New York fur traders continue to move into New France.

——————— 1763 ———————

On February 10, the Treaty of Paris ends the Seven Years' War, resulting in the withdrawal of French government from Quebec. Henley House is opened for trade for the third time.

——————— 1765 ———————

Bibye Lake is appointed HBC Deputy Governor. The HBC starts a whale fishery on Marble Island, 250 miles north of Fort Prince of Wales.

——————— 1767 ———————

Hearne finds the remains of the James Knight expedition on Marble Island.

——————— 1768 ———————

Imperial regulations are relaxed to promote Quebec trade, and Montreal merchants are allowed to trade in the "North West" but not in Rupert's Land; huge decline in HBC trade due to the competitiveness of the Montreal-based "pedlars."

——————— 1769 ———————

Samuel Hearne sets out on his first journey to the Coppermine River but is forced back short of his goal.

——————— 1770 ———————

Hearne sets off again on February 23, travels about three hundred miles but is compelled to return to Fort Prince of Wales yet again. Bibye Lake, another son of Sir Bibye Lake, is appointed HBC Governor.

——————— 1771 ———————

Hearne finally reaches the Coppermine River on July 12, is shaken by the massacre at Bloody Fall on July 17 and reaches the Arctic at Coronation Gulf on July 18.

——————— 1772 ———————

The HBC sends Matthew Cocking from York Factory to check on the pedlars dominating the fur trade by

using tobacco and liquor as trade items. Hearne arrives back at Fort Prince of Wales on June 30.

——————— 1774 ———————

Hearne builds the first inland HBC post at Cumberland House, near Pine Island Lake on the Saskatchewan River.

——————— 1775 ———————

War breaks out in the Thirteen Colonies. Simon McTavish moves to Montreal from Albany. Hearne, thirty, is appointed commander of Fort Prince of Wales.

——————— 1776 ———————

The "pedlars" regroup in Montreal, sometimes using the name North West Company; they establish their main supply base at Grand Portage at the western end of Lake Superior.

——————— 1778 ———————

Peter Pond, exploring the Athabasca Delta for the North West Co., spots oil sands and rich furs and establishes a post.

——————— 1779 ———————

The "pedlars" in Montreal form a sixteen-share partnership of merchants, but the North West Company is restructured three times before emerging in 1783 as a permanent entity.

——————— 1780 ———————

Thomas Empson makes the first point blankets for the HBC, each "point," a small, dark mark woven into the wool, representing the value of one beaver pelt (a made beaver). Both the HBC and NWC begin establishing inland posts in fierce competition for the fur trade.

——————— 1781–1782 ———————

Smallpox kills many Plains Indians.

——————— 1782 ———————

Fort Prince of Wales at Churchill River is captured by Admiral La Pérouse on August 9 and is destroyed; Samuel Hearne is taken prisoner; York Factory surrenders on August 25.

——————— 1786 ———————

HBC appoints William Tomison chief at York Factory, with responsibility for inland posts. "Most likely date" for George Simpson's birth.

——————— 1789 ———————

Alexander Mackenzie sets off from Fort Chipewyan on June 3 to explore "the Grand River" (later the Mackenzie) and on July 14 reaches the Arctic Ocean.

——————— 1790 ———————

McTavish, Frobisher & Co. dominates the newly formed North West partnership, with Simon McTavish holding controlling interest. Philip Turnor, HBC surveyor, arrives ill-equipped in Athabasca and hears Indians' complaints re NWC traders.

——————— 1793 ———————

Alexander Mackenzie, NWC partner, sets out on May 9 to find a river route to the Pacific; he reaches the ocean July 21 at Dean Channel. The Nor'Westers now control 78 percent of Canadian fur sales.

——————— 1794 ———————

Intense feuding surfaces between Alexander Mackenzie and Simon McTavish; Mackenzie wants merger of NWC with the HBC. Fort Edmonton is established by William Tomison, Inland Chief of the HBC, near the older NWC Fort Augustus.

——————— 1797 ———————

David Thompson defects from the HBC to the NWC. Russian-American Company is formed to trade in furs from Alaska.

——————— 1798 ———————

Breakaway Montreal traders coalesce as the New North West Company, dubbed the XY Company.

——————— 1799 ———————

Sir James Winter Lake, son of Sir Atwell Lake, is appointed Governor. Despite rapid expansion, the HBC has only 498 men posted in North America. The Nor'Westers build a wooden canal to bypass the portage at Sault Ste Marie. Mackenzie and McTavish square off in a power play at the NWC annual conclave; Mackenzie loses. Upon his father's death, Thomas Douglas becomes the 5th Earl of Selkirk.

——————— 1800 ———————

Alexander Mackenzie joins the XY Company, which becomes popularly known as "Alexander Mackenzie & Co."

Alexander Mackenzie is knighted by George III and very nearly gains control of the HBC. HBC's Peter Fidler, assigned to establish Nottingham House post near Fort Chipewyan, is harassed by Nor'Westers Archibald Norman McLeod and Samuel Black.

——— 1803 ———

NWC headquarters is moved from Grand Portage, which has become U.S. territory, to Fort William. British Parliament on Aug. 11 passes the Canada Jurisdiction Act aimed at regulating lawless conflict between HBC and NWC. NWC's McTavish establishes four outlaw posts on Hudson Bay; they last three years.

——— 1804 ———

U.S. President Thomas Jefferson dispatches Lewis and Clark expedition to the Pacific Coast. Lord Selkirk visits Montreal. Simon McTavish of the NWC, foe of the XY Company's Alexander Mackenzie, dies on July 6; NWC and XY Company agree to merge, Nov 5.

——— 1804–1821 ———

The NWC consistently ships more furs than the HBC, yet both sides suffer losses and low profits due to increased costs, overtrapping and fierce competition.

——— 1805 ———

Meriwether Lewis and William Clark reach the Pacific Ocean, overland, on Nov. 14. Mackenzie, who had reached the Pacific in July 1793, leaves Montreal to live in Britain.

——— 1806 ———

At the annual Fort William conclave, a new resolution is adopted prohibiting Nor'Westers from taking Indian wives. HBC servants have by now opened sixty inland stations.

——— 1807 ———

William Mainwaring is appointed Governor of the HBC. David Thompson, his wife and family cross the Rockies on mapmaking journey. Selkirk marries Jean Wedderburn.

——— 1808 ———

May-June-July: Simon Fraser makes his 850-mile journey to the Pacific down the river now named for him.

——— 1809 ———

Andrew Colvile reorganizes the financially sluggish HBC to combat the NWC competition, as proposed by Colin Robertson; masters of HBC posts are given increased flexibility and power in trade, and a share in profits. NWC builds Fort Gibraltar on the future site of Winnipeg. Between 1809 and 1815, the HBC pays no dividends.

——— 1811 ———

Lord Selkirk, major HBC stockholder, on March 6 reaches agreement to buy more than 74 million acres, or 116,000 square miles, for 10 shillings to establish a settlement at Red River; on July 26, the first shipload of settlers is under way. Great flood of the Red River. John Jacob Astor's men establish Astoria at the mouth of the Columbia River in March; the NWC's David Thompson arrives there in mid-July. HBC profits are £57,860, compared with a loss of £19,000 in 1809.

——— 1812 ———

U.S. declares war on Britain and closes border. Joseph Berens, Jr., is appointed HBC Governor. On July 17, the British seize Michilimackinac from the Americans with the help of NWC voyageurs. On Aug. 30, Miles Macdonell and first settlers reach Red River. On Oct. 1, the Corps of Canadian Voyageurs is formed; is disbanded March 14, 1813. Cuthbert Grant, at nineteen, is sent out to the Qu'Appelle River as an NWC clerk.

——— 1813 ———

NWC lays siege to, then buys, Astoria. It is then officially proclaimed British by Capt. Black of HMS Racoon.

——— 1814 ———

Demand for fur revives on London markets. The Treaty of Ghent defines the boundary between Canada and the United States. John McLoughlin, physician at Fort William, is named an NWC partner.

——— 1815 ———

Red River Governor Miles Macdonell surrenders himself to the NWC at Fort Gibraltar; most settlers abandon Red River after houses are burned, but return to their farms after meeting HBC Chief Factor Colin Robertson en route to Athabasca. Robert Semple is appointed new Governor of Red River. Selkirk receives initial proposal from William McGillivray re HBC-NWC amalgamation.

——— 1816 ———

Former Nor'Wester John Clarke leads HBC brigade into Athabasca. Ill-equipped and faced with NWC hostility, sixteen men starve. The first permanent HBC post of the Athabasca Country, Fort Wedderburn, opens. On June 19, Semple and twenty others are shot and their bodies mutilated at Seven Oaks by a troop of NWC adherents led by Cuthbert Grant. Settlers flee. Selkirk and his mercenaries seize Fort William on August 12 and arrest several NWC partners for their complicity in the massacre. Severe cold spells mark this a "year without a summer."

——— 1817 ———

Lord Selkirk stays thirteen summer weeks at the Red River Colony. Royal proclamation is made on May 1 against "open warfare in the Indian territories."

——— 1818 ———

On October 11 in the Athabasca Country, the HBC's Colin Robertson is kidnapped by Nor'Wester Samuel Black. Selkirk is embroiled in court challenges to his Red River aspirations.

——— 1819 ———

Post-war depression hits British North America and the U.S. Selkirk leaves England in September for Pau, France.

——— 1820 ———

Lord Selkirk and Alexander Mackenzie die within twenty-seven days of each other. Colvile dispatches George Simpson to Rupert's Land; Simpson sets out overseas to Montreal, Fort William and Athabasca. John McLoughlin and Angus Bethune head via Montreal to London to negotiate on behalf of the NWC's unhappy wintering partners.

——————— 1821 ———————

On March 26, the amalgamation agreement between the HBC and NWC is signed; the British Parliament on July 2 grants the combined companies under the HBC name a twenty-one-year monopoly over the fur trade in British North America west of Upper Canada; HBC now controls more than 3 million square miles of land, and amalgamation of the two companies' 173 posts begins. The NWC wintering partners converge on Fort William on July 10 to learn of the changes. The HBC men converge on Norway House, and HBC Committeeman Nicholas Garry presents the new arrangements. George Simpson becomes Governor of the new Northern Department. Traders of both companies later meet at York Factory. Swiss settlers arrive at the Selkirk Settlement, but most soon leave for the U.S. Alexander I of Russia issues an imperial edict restricting shipping and fur trading on the northwest coast of North America.

——————— 1822 ———————

John Henry Pelly is appointed Governor of the HBC. Simpson embarks on snowshoe trek across the Athabasca, Slave and Peace regions. HBC forms the Buffalo Wool Co., which fails, as do the later tallow export and sheep wool companies.

——————— 1823 ———————

John Rowand establishes HBC's North-west headquarters at Fort Edmonton, near the present Alberta Legislature.

——————— 1824 ———————

Simpson appoints John McLoughlin Chief Factor of the Columbia Department, and visits Astoria. Headquarters is moved from Astoria to Fort Vancouver, a hundred miles up the Columbia River. A chain of posts is eventually established from the Columbia north to Alaska, and the shoreline is patrolled by Company vessels. Anglo-Russian Treaty fixes boundary of Alaska at 54°40'. James Douglas marries Amelia Connolly. The

original profit-sharing agreement of the 1821 amalgamation agreement falls apart; former NWC agents lose their votes and influence in HBC affairs, and must post bond to cover legal expenses. In the 1824 reorganization, former Nor'West agent Edward Ellice joins the HBC's Committee and continues to prosper, unlike his former NWC colleagues.

——————— 1825 ———————

William McGillivray dies, leaving his brother Simon with onerous debts.

——————— 1826 ———————

George Simpson is officially named Governor of both the Northern and Southern departments. Severe flood at Red River.

——————— 1828 ———————

HBC dividends reach 20 percent, up from 4 percent in 1824. Simpson again ventures to the Pacific. Cuthbert Grant is named Warden of the Plains by Simpson.

——————— 1830 ———————

Simpson marries his cousin Frances and honeymoons in a canoe.

——————— 1831 ———————

Construction begins on Lower Fort Garry.

——————— 1832 ———————

The Simpsons move into Lower Fort Garry (the "Stone Fort").

——————— 1833 ———————

Simpson transfers management operations to Lachine; Frances returns to England, until 1845.

——————— 1835–1837 ———————

Upper Fort Garry is started in 1835 to replace an older fort damaged in 1826 flooding. Smallpox on the Plains; by 1837 an estimated three-quarters of the Plains Indians die.

——————— 1836 ———————

HBC steamer *Beaver* goes into service on Pacific Coast. Selkirk family on May 4 trades its lands for £84,000 worth of HBC stock. Upper Fort Garry becomes the administrative centre of Assiniboia.

——————— 1837 ———————

Economic depression hits low point.

——————— 1838 ———————

HBC licensed monopoly is renewed for another twenty-one years by the British government. Simpson travels to St. Petersburg. Samuel Black, former tormentor of HBC men, is named one of the Company's chief factors.

——————— 1839 ———————

Andrew Colvile becomes HBC Deputy Governor. Simpson is appointed Governor-in-Chief of Rupert's Land. James Douglas is appointed Chief Factor of the Columbia Department.

——————— 1840 ———————

Red River's population has increased to 4,369 from less than 300 in 1818. John Henry Pelly is created a baronet.

——————— 1841–1842 ———————

Simpson is knighted; he circles the world, from London, via Halifax, Boston, Montreal, Fort Vancouver, California, Hawaii, Alaska, Siberia and Europe; nineteen months, nineteen days later, he is back in London. Upper Canada is renamed Canada West; Lower Canada becomes Canada East. Limits are imposed on the beaver catch in the interests of conservation.

——————— 1843 ———————

Fort Victoria is established by James Douglas at the southern tip of Vancouver Island. Final HBC anti-liquor regulation is approved by Council at Red River on June 17. Norman Kittson attempts to lure fur trade from Fort Garry to his U.S. post at Pembina.

——————— 1846 ———————

Oregon Treaty establishes the 49th parallel as the boundary between American and British territory west of the Rockies, with Vancouver Island to be British.

——————— 1849 ———————

Sayer Trial at Red River opens the market for free traders in fur. Cuthbert Grant is fired by Simpson. Andrew Colvile's son Eden is named Associate Governor of Rupert's Land. Richard Blanshard is appointed Governor of the Colony of Vancouver Island, granted to the HBC by the British government.

—————— 1851 ——————
James Douglas is appointed Governor of Vancouver Island, following Richard Blanshard's resignation.

—————— 1852 ——————
Sir John Pelly dies, and Andrew Colvile, HBC Deputy Governor since 1839, is appointed Governor.

—————— 1853 ——————
Frances Simpson dies.

—————— 1856 ——————
John Shepherd is appointed Governor of the HBC.

—————— 1857 ——————
HBC licence comes due for renewal. Parliamentary hearings inquire into the HBC's position and practices. David Thompson dies impoverished in Longueuil.

—————— 1858 ——————
Colony of British Columbia is created. Discovery of gold on the Fraser River attracts a rush of Americans into British territory. Henry Hulse Berens is appointed Governor of the HBC.

—————— 1859 ——————
HBC has retained its territorial rights but has lost its licence to exclusive trade. The *Anson Northup* reaches Fort Garry from Minnesota on June 10. First major Canadian rail project, the Grand Trunk, is completed between Lévis, opposite Quebec City, and Sarnia.

—————— 1860 ——————
Simpson entertains the Prince of Wales in Lachine on Aug. 29, dies on Sept. 7. Alexander Grant Dallas succeeds him and moves headquarters from Lachine to Red River. United States has 30,000 route-miles of rail track. Gold fever pulls miners to the Cariboo Country.

—————— 1862 ——————
Simon Fraser dies destitute. British Crown takes back from the HBC all rights over Vancouver Island.

—————— 1863 ——————
Edward Watkin, supported by the International Financial Society of London, buys out all HBC stock on June 15. The London Committee is reorganized; Sir Edmund Walker Head is appointed HBC Governor.

James Douglas is knighted by Queen Victoria.

—————— 1864 ——————
Negotiations towards Confederation of Canada take place in Quebec City and Charlottetown.

—————— 1866 ——————
U.S. allows 1854 Reciprocity Treaty to lapse; Canadian economy suffers severe recession. Fenians raid northward across the Canada-U.S. border.

—————— 1867 ——————
The British North America Act creating Canada is enacted at Westminster on March 29; Clause 146 makes provision for the admission of Rupert's Land and Northwest Territories into the new Confederation.

—————— 1868 ——————
The Earl of Kimberley is appointed Governor of the HBC. Canadian delegation arrives in London to begin negotiations for HBC lands.

—————— 1869 ——————
HBC signs Deed of Surrender on November 19, agreeing to surrender Rupert's Land to the Crown. HBC gains cash settlement, and keeps its 120 posts and land concessions. William McDougall, appointed Lieutenant-Governor of Rupert's Land and the Northwest Territories, sets out for Red River; is turned back at Pembina by armed Métis.

—————— 1870 ——————
Sir Stafford Northcote, later Earl of Iddesleigh, is appointed Governor of the HBC. Northern Department of Rupert's Land holds its final meeting at Norway House. Rebellion at Red River under Louis Riel. The HBC's Chief Commissioner Donald Smith assures Louis Riel of Canada's good intentions. As a result, Métis form a provisional government to negotiate with Ottawa.

—————— 1871 ——————
Final York boat brigade arrives at York Factory.

—————— 1875 ——————
Upper Fort Garry becomes the headquarters of the Northern Department.

—————— 1885 ——————
Louis Riel hanged at Regina for high treason after Northwest Rebellion of that year.

—————— 1886–1887 ——————
During the winter, tribes starve in the Northwest "owing to the destruction of game."

—————— 1887 ——————
No further commissioned officers are appointed by the HBC.

—————— 1889 ——————
Donald Smith is appointed Governor of the HBC.

—————— 1897 ——————
Donald Smith is elevated to the peerage as Lord Strathcona and Mount Royal.

—————— Early 1900s ——————
More than three million immigrants settle the Prairies between 1900 and 1914. The old HBC posts evolve into saleshops in growing western cities.

—————— 1910–1914 ——————
HBC rushes to build or expand department stores in Vancouver, Calgary, Edmonton and Victoria.

—————— 1912 ——————
First HBC management advisory group appointed in Winnipeg.

—————— 1913 ——————
HBC pays dividend of 50%.

—————— 1914 ——————
Lord Strathcona dies.

—————— 1915–1919 ——————
London's HBC office expanded into war service as overseas purchasing agent for the French Government, chartering a merchant fleet of 300 vessels, to transport foodstuffs, fuel, lumber and munitions.

—————— May 2, 1920 ——————
The 250th anniversary of the HBC.

—————— 1920 ——————
HBC opens a Newfoundland fishing and packing industry. Offices opened in Paris and New York.

—————— 1926 ——————
Construction starts on Beaver House. World's largest fur auction trade house built in London. HBC agreement with Marland Oil Co. of Oklahoma to explore large freehold mineral rights in western Canada.

1927
First two northern air-freight planes sent to Churchill by James Richardson of the HBC Canadian Committee. Two railways reach the shores of Hudson Bay.

1929
Marland merged into Continental Oil (backed by J. P. Morgan) and Hudson's Bay Oil and Gas Company formed.

1938
Dividends resumed after a lapse of seven years during the Depression.

1945
HBC shows highest profit to date.

1947
Hudson's Bay Oil & Gas reactivated.

1950–1970
Hudson's Bay Oil & Gas Company enjoys prolific gas discoveries.

1960
HBC buys the ten-unit chain of Montreal's Henry Morgan department stores.

1962
Hudson's Bay Oil & Gas Company has a major gas strike at Kaybob South, north of Edmonton — the largest gas field in Canada.

1965
The HBC becomes "The Bay" — a change in their public image.

1967
More than 80% of HBC shareholders are still UK residents. New department stores are planned to 1985 at the rate of two or three a year.

1968
Hudson's Bay Oil & Gas Company files on 1.2 million acres in the Beaufort Sea to explore for oil.

1969
Hudson's Bay Oil & Gas Company acquires land in the Arctic.

May 2, 1970
300th anniversary. HBC announces move of its headquarters from London to Winnipeg.

1972
HBC purchases the five-store Freiman's chain in Ottawa.

1978
HBC takes over Zellers and Simpsons department store chains.

1978-1979
The Bay jumps from the 22nd-largest corporation in Canada to the 10th.

1978
Ken Thomson purchases 76% of the HBC's outstanding shares for $640 million cash.

1980
HBC pays $32 million for 60% equity interest in Roxy Petroleum Ltd.

1981
Ranked 10th-largest among Canadian corporations, the HBC employs more than 42,000 people, has major interests in gas, oil and land development, and is still the world's largest fur-trading company.

1987
HBC sells its northern stores, fur auction houses and Roxy Petroleum.

1990
48 Towers discount stores acquired and converted to Zellers stores.

1991
HBC shuts down its unsuccessful Simpsons division. Seven stores are merged with the Bay; the remainder sold to Sears.

1992
Thomson family reduce their stake in HBC to 23%, leaving the company without a majority shareholder.

1993
HBC takes over Vancouver-based Woodward's department store chain.

1995
HBC celebrates its 325th anniversary.

BIBLIOGRAPHY

Beattie, Owen B., and John Geiger. *Frozen in Time: Unlocking the Secrets of the Franklin Expedition*. Saskatoon: Western Producer Prairie Books, 1988.

Berton, Pierre. *The Arctic Grail: The Quest for the North West Passage and the North Pole, 1818–1909*. Toronto: McClelland & Stewart, 1988.

Francis, Daniel. *The Battle for the West: Fur Traders and the Birth of Western Canada*. Edmonton: Hurtig, 1982.

Grant, Hugh. "The Revenge of the Paris Hat." *The Beaver*, December 1988–January 1989: 37–44.

Harris, R. Cole, Editor, and Geoffrey J. Matthews, Cartographer and Designer. *Historical Atlas of Canada*. Volume I, *From the Beginning to 1800*. Toronto: University of Toronto Press, 1987.

Newman, Peter C. *Company of Adventurers*. Volume II, *Caesars of the Wilderness*. Toronto: Penguin, 1987.

Newman, Peter C. "The Hudson's Bay Company: Canada's Fur-Trading Empire." *National Geographic*, August 1987: 192–229.

Prebble, John. *The Highland Clearances*. New York: Penguin, 1967.

Rasky, Frank. *The Taming of the Canadian West*. Toronto: McClelland & Stewart, 1967.

Rich, E. E. *History of the Hudson's Bay Company, 1670–1870*. Volume I, 1670–1763 (HBRS, Vol. 21); Volume 2, 1763–1870 (HBRS, Vol. 22). London: Hudson's Bay Record Society, 1958, 1959.

Tanner, Ogden. *The Canadians*. Old West Series. Alexandria, Virginia: Time-Life Books, 1977.

Williams, Glyndwr. "The Hudson's Bay Company and the Fur Trade." *The Beaver*, August 1983: 4–82.

ILLUSTRATION CREDITS

Cover *Canoe Manned by Voyageurs* by Frances Ann Hopkins. National Archives of Canada (C-2771).

Endpapers *The Cataract of Niagara...A View of ye Industry of ye Beavers of Canada in making Dams...*by H. Moll. National Archives of Canada (C-16758).
2 Hudson's Bay Company.
3-4 Kevin Fleming.
7-8 *Canoe Party around Campfire* by Frances Ann Hopkins. National Archives of Canada (C-2772).
9 Kevin Fleming.
10-11 Kevin Fleming.
12 Hudson's Bay Company Archives, Provincial Archives of Manitoba (1987/363/B-20).
14 National Archives of Canada (C-99255).
15 *Running a Rapid on the Mattawa River* by C. Butterworth (after Mrs. F.A. Hopkins). National Archives of Canada (C-13585).
16 National Archives of Canada (PA-101856).
17 Kevin Fleming.
18-19 Jack McMaster.
20 (Upper) *Modifications of the Beaver Hat.* National Archives of Canada (C-17338). (Lower) *The Beaver.*
20-21 Kevin Fleming.
21 (Upper) *The Beaver.* (Lower) *The Beaver.*
22 *Hudson's Bay Company Ketch the* Nonsuch by Mark Richard Myers. Hudson's Bay Company Archives, Provincial Archives of Manitoba (P-210).
24 *Englishmen in a Skirmish with Eskimos* by John White, ca. 1590. Trustees of the British Museum.
25 *Map of Hudson Bay and Straits* by Samuel Thornton. Hudson's Bay Company Archives, Provincial Archives of Manitoba (Map G.2/2).
27 *The Last Voyage* by John Collier. The Tate Gallery, London (N1616).
28 *Henry Hudson. The Celebrated and Unfortunate Navigator Abandoned By His Crew in Hudson's Bay the 11th of June 1610* by F. Davignon. Royal Ontario Museum (748.276.3).
29 "Jens Munk's Winter-Haven" Hudson's Bay Company Archives, Provincial Archives of Manitoba.
30 (Upper) Jack McMaster. (Lower) *Pierre-Esprit Radisson* by Belier. National Archives of Canada (C-15497).

31 *Radisson & Grosseilliers* by Frederic Remington. Remington Museum, Ogdensburg, New York.
33 Kevin Fleming.
35 *Nonsuch Enroute to Hudson's Bay* by Norman Wilkinson. Hudson's Bay Company Archives, Provincial Archives of Manitoba (P-446).
36 (Upper) *Nonsuch* diagram sideview by Adrian Small. Hudson's Bay Company Archives, Provincial Archives of Manitoba (N-18, 75-7). (Lower) *Nonsuch* diagram cross-section. Hudson's Bay Company Archives, Provincial Archives of Manitoba (N-18).
37 Franz Rosenbaum.
38 *The Nonsuch Arrives in London, October 1669* by Norman Wilkinson. Hudson's Bay Company Archives, Provincial Archives of Manitoba (P-409).
40 *Signing of the HBC Charter By Charles II on May 2nd, 1670.* Hudson's Bay Company Archives, Provincial Archives of Manitoba (P-379).
41 *The First Public Sale of Furs, 1672* by Edward North (after Alfred Cooke and Son). Hudson's Bay Company Archives, Provincial Archives of Manitoba (C.69 1918).
43-44 Kevin Fleming.
44 (Inset) Kevin Fleming.
44 *Duke of Marlborough* by Sir John Lely. Hudson's Bay Company Archives, Provincial Archives of Manitoba (1987/363/M-15).
45 *A South View of Albany Factory, a Winter View* by William Richards. Hudson's Bay Company Archives, Provincial Archives of Manitoba (P-118).
48 (Upper) "Bombardment of York Factory" from *Histoire de l'Amerique Septentrionale,* Vol. 1 (Paris, 1753) by Bacqueville de La Potherie. Hudson's Bay Company Archives, Provincial Archives of Manitoba (1987/363/Y-100). (Lower) National Archives of Canada (C-26026).
49 *The Battle in the Bay, 1697* by Norman Wilkinson. Hudson's Bay Company Archives, Provincial Archives of Manitoba (P-401).
51 Kevin Fleming.
50-51 York Factory 1853 from a lithograph supposed to have been done from a sketch by Alexander Hamilton Murray. Hudson's

Bay Company Archives, Provincial Archives of Manitoba (P-114).
51 (Upper) Kevin Fleming. (Lower) National Archives of Canada (PA-123668).
52 *Prince of Wales's Fort* by A.H. Hider (from a steel engraving by Samuel Hearne). Hudson's Bay Company Archives, Provincial Archives of Manitoba (1987/363/C.69 1922).
54 Hudson's Bay Company Archives, Provincial Archives of Manitoba (RBFC3212C5).
55 "The Wintering Creek in Hayes River" from *A Voyage to Hudson's Bay* by Henry Ellis. Hudson's Bay Company Archives, Provincial Archives of Manitoba.
56 "Crossing Mosquito Lake" from *Explorations in the Interior of the Labrador Peninsula.* Metropolitan Toronto Library.
57 *Sailing of the Hudson's Bay Company Ships from Gravesend, 8th June, 1845.* Hudson's Bay Company Archives, Provincial Archives of Manitoba (P-158).
58 (Upper) "An Xmas Ball in Bachelor's Hall, York Factory, 1843" from *Hudson's Bay; or, Everyday Life in the Wilds of North America.* Hudson's Bay Company Archives, Provincial Archives of Manitoba. (Middle) Hudson's Bay Company Archives, Provincial Archives of Manitoba (1987/363/N-41). (Lower) Kevin Fleming.
59 (Upper) Kevin Fleming. (Lower) "Arrival of Hudson's Bay Company Ships" from *Picturesque Canada,* Vol. 1 (Toronto, 1882). National Archives of Canada (C-82981). (Lower right) Kevin Fleming.
60 *Indians Trading Furs, 1785* by C.W. Jefferys. National Archives of Canada (C-73431).
60-61 See Spot Run.
61 Kevin Fleming.
62 National Archives of Canada (C-3280).
62 Line drawing by Pronk&Associates.
63 Kevin Fleming.
65 *Kelsey Sees the Buffalo, August 1691* by C.W. Jefferys. Hudson's Bay Company Archives, Provincial Archives of Manitoba (1987/363/C.69 1928).
66 *Ambassadress of Peace* by Franklin Arbuckle. Hudson's Bay Company Archives, Provincial Archives of Manitoba (1987/363/C.69 1953).
68 (Upper) "The Fall in the Upper Part of Wager Bay" from *A Voyage to Hudson's*

218

Bay by Henry Ellis. Hudson's Bay Company Archives, Provincial Archives of Manitoba. (Lower) *The Governor Arthur Dobbs.* North Carolina State Archives.

70 "A New Chart of Where a North West Passage Was Sought" from *A Voyage to Hudson's Bay* by Henry Ellis.

71 (Upper) Kevin Fleming. (Lower left) Hudson's Bay Company Archives/Provincial Archives of Manitoba (E.2/2 fo.21). (Lower right) Kevin Fleming.

72 (Upper) Kevin Fleming. (Lower) Kevin Fleming.

73 (Upper) *A Man and His Wife Returning with a Load of Partridges from Their Tent* by William Richards. Hudson's Bay Company Archives, Provincial Archives of Manitoba (P-116). (Lower) Kevin Fleming.

74 *Henday Enters the Blackfoot Camp* by Franklin Arbuckle. Hudson's Bay Company Archives, Provincial Archives of Manitoba (1987/363/C.69 1951).

76 *Rival Traders Racing to the Indian Camp* by Frederic Remington. National Archives of Canada (C-747).

78 *Mr. Samuel Hearne, late Chief at Prince of Wales's Fort, Hudson's Bay, 1796* by unknown artist. Hudson's Bay Company Archives, Provincial Archives of Manitoba (P-167).

79 National Archives of Canada (C-70644).

81 Map from *Journey to the Northern Sea* by Samuel Hearne. Metropolitan Toronto Library (917.12427).

83 Kevin Fleming.

84 Jack McMaster.

85 "A Winter View of Athapuscow Lake" from *Journey to the Northern Sea* by Samuel Hearne. Hudson's Bay Company Archives, Provincial Archives of Manitoba (1987/363/E-700H).

86 (Inset) *A Hunter-family of Cree Indians at York Fort, Drawn from Nature* by Peter Rindisbacher. National Archives of Canada (C-1917).

86-87 Kevin Fleming.

88 *The Rendezvous* by A.J. Miller. National Archives of Canada (C-439).

89 (Upper) New York Historical Society (41509). (Lower) Identified on Painting as "Fort Garry, Winnipeg" by W. Frank Lynn. Hudson's Bay Company Archives, Provincial Archives of Manitoba.

90 *Making Presents to Blackfoot Indians* by A.J. Miller. Walters Art Gallery, Baltimore (37 1940 13 C82).

95 (Upper) *Mr. Samuel Hearne, late Chief at Prince of Wales's Fort, Hudson's Bay, 1796* by unknown artist. Hudson's Bay Company Archives, Provincial Archives of Manitoba (P-167). (Lower) Kevin Fleming.

96 (Upper) Hudson's Bay Company Archives, Provincial Archives of Manitoba (G.2/5). (Lower) Kevin Fleming.

97 (Upper) *A South-West View of Prince of Wales' Fort after a Drawing by Samuel Hearne.* Metropolitan Toronto Library (MTL 2249). (Lower) Kevin Fleming.

98 National Archives of Canada (C-164).

99 Hudson's Bay Company Archives, Provincial Archives of Manitoba (B.39/a/22 fo.69).

102-103 Kevin Fleming.

102 (Inset) Kevin Fleming.

103 (Inset) *Alexander Mackenzie* by Sir Thomas Lawrence. The National Gallery of Canada (8000), Ottawa.

104 *David Thompson in the Athabasca Pass, 1810* by C.W. Jefferys. National Archives of Canada (C-70258).

105 Oregon Historical Society (ORHI 21682 and ORHI 60033).

107 Jack McMaster.

108 (Upper) National Archives of Canada (C-21522). (Lower) Kevin Fleming. (Lower, inset) *The Governor of Red River Voyaging in a Light Canoe* by H. Jones (after Peter Rindisbacher). National Archives of Canada (C-1944).

108 Kevin Fleming.

110-111 *Shooting the Rapids* by Frances Ann Hopkins. National Archives of Canada (C-2774).

112 (Upper) *Canadian Voyageurs in Captain Franklin's Canoe* by Captain Basil Hill. National Archives of Canada (C-9461). (Lower) Kevin Fleming.

113 *At the Portage* by H.A. Ogden. National Archives of Canada (C-82974).

114-115 *Voyageurs at Dawn, 1871* by Frances Ann Hopkins. National Archives of Canada (C-2773).

116 *Settler's House and Red River Cart, Manitoba* by William G.R. Hind. National Archives of Canada (C-13965).

111 National Archives of Canada (C-1346).

121 *Buffalo Meat Drying* by William Armstrong. National Archives of Canada (C-10502).

122 National Archives of Canada (C-624).

123 National Archives of Canada (C-8984).

125 *Seven Oaks Massacre* by C.W. Jefferys. National Archives of Canada (C-73663).

126 (Upper) Oregon Historical Society (ORHI 248).

126-127 Province of Ontario.

127 (Upper left) *Maclean's* April 30, 1955. Toronto Star Syndicate. (Upper right) National Archives of Canada (C-8711).

128 Provincial Archives of Ontario (MH 3279 1367).

129 National Archives of Canada. (C-19202).

130 (Upper) Mitchell Library, Glasgow. (Lower) *Last of the Clan* by John Faed. Glasgow Art Gallery.

131 Tim Ball.

132 (Upper) *Departure of the Second Colonist Transport from York Fort to Rockfort, September 6, 1821* by Peter Rindisbacher. National Archives of Canada (C-1918). (Lower) Glenbow Museum (63.37.13).

133 (Upper) Hudson's Bay Company Archives, Provincial Archives of Manitoba (1987/363/R13.1). (Lower left) Selkirk Land Grant (Penguin). (Lower right) *Colonists from Red River* by Peter Rindisbacher. National Archives of Canada (C-1937).

134 *Hudson's Bay House, No. 3 and 4 Fenchurch Street* by Thomas Colman Dibdin. Hudson's Bay Company Archives, Provincial Archives of Manitoba (P-220).

136 National Archives of Canada (C-2385).

137 National Archives of Canada (C-176).

138 McCord Museum (M-18683).

139 Provincial Archives of Manitoba.

141 *George Simpson's Canoe at Fort William* by William Armstrong. Royal Ontario Museum (979.64.1).

142 Provincial Archives of British Columbia (HP2656).

143 Engraving by James Scott. Hudson's Bay Company Archives, Provincial Archives of Manitoba (P-204).

145 *Captain Franklin R.N., F.R.S. Commander of the Land Arctic Expedition.* Royal Ontario Museum (970.21.1).

145 *First Winter in the Ice at Beechey Island.* Royal Ontario Museum (955.141.1).

146 *Abandoning the Ships.* Royal Ontario Museum (955.141.3).

146 *Sledges in Fresh Fair Wind, Going over Hummocky Ice.* Royal Ontario Museum (960.604).

146 *Sir John Franklin's Last Expedition.* Royal Ontario Museum (955.141.2).

146 *H.M.S. Terror as She Appeared after Being Thrown up by the Ice on September 27th, 1836* by Lieutenant William Smith. Hudson's Bay Company Archives, Provincial Archives of Manitoba (P-215).

147 *Portrait of John Rae in Arctic Garb, 1862* by William Armstrong. Glenbow Museum (Cat. no. Aw. 55.17.1, Photo no. 1162).

147 Painting by Charles Comfort. Hudson's Bay Company Archives, Provincial Archives of Manitoba (1987/363/R-2).

148 (Upper) *Franklin Relics Brought by Doctor Rae* by Commander W.W. May. Royal Ontario Museum (954.44.1M). (Lower) *Illustrated London News* October 4, 1851.

149 (Upper left) Hudson's Bay Company Archives, Provincial Archives of Manitoba (A-389). (Upper right) *Illustrated London News* October 15, 1859. (Lower) Owen Beattie.

151 *HBC York Boats at Norway House* by W.J. Phillips. Hudson's Bay Company Archives, Provincial Archives of Manitoba (1987/363/C.69 1930).

152-153 *Brigade of Boats* by Paul Kane. Royal Ontario Museum (912.1.31).

154 (Upper) Provincial Archives of Alberta (B2911). (Middle) Provincial Archives of Alberta (B2912). (Lower) Provincial Archives of Alberta (B2910).

154-155 Kevin Fleming.

156 Kevin Fleming.

158 Engraving by A. Rochester Fellow. Provincial Archives of Manitoba (N10299).

159 Hudson's Bay Company Archives, Provincial Archives of Manitoba (P-225).

160 *The Trapper's Bride* by A.J. Miller. Jocelyn Art Museum (1963.612).

161 (Upper) Provincial Archives of British Columbia (HP-2659). (Lower) *The Governor of Red River, Driving his Family on the River in a Horse Cariole* by H. Jones (copied from Peter Rindisbacher). Hudson's Bay Company Archives, Provincial Archives of Manitoba (P-183).

164 Hudson's Bay Company Archives, Provincial Archives of Manitoba (1987/363/S-25).

165 *Illustrated London News* October 13, 1861.

167 Hudson's Bay Company Archives, Provincial Archives of Manitoba (P-200).

168 Hudson's Bay Company Archives, Provincial Archives of Manitoba (1987/363/H-3).
170 Bettmann Archive (F5217).
171 (Upper) National Archives of Canada (C-1229). (Middle) National Archives of Canada (C-16441). (Lower) Provincial Archives of Alberta (B2917).
172 (Upper) Kevin Fleming. (Lower) Notman Photographic Archives (A5396).
173 Kevin Fleming.
174-175 *Fort Edmonton* by Paul Kane. Royal Ontario Museum. (Upper) Provincial Archives of Alberta (B6580). (Lower) National Archives of Canada (PA-9240).
175 Provincial Archives of Alberta (B6637).
176 Notman Photographic Archives (LL0, 266-11).
178 Notman Photographic Archives (4267).
180 Metropolitan Toronto Library (T33162).
181 Provincial Archives of Manitoba (N5732).
182 (Upper) Provincial Archives of Alberta (A8102).(Lower) Provincial Archives of Alberta (A8101).
183 (Upper) Provincial Archives of Alberta (B4424). (Lower) Provincial Archives of Alberta (B5184).
184 Notman Photographic Archives (MP296B).
185 Hudson's Bay Company Archives, Provincial Archives of Manitoba (P-168).
187 Hudson's Bay Company Archives, Provincial Archives of Manitoba (P-204).

188–189 *The HB Company Ships Prince of Wales and Eddystone Bartering with the Eskimos off the Upper Savage Islands, Hudson Strait, NWT* by Robert Hood. National Archives of Canada (C-40364).
190 (Upper) Vancouver City Archives. (Lower) Hudson's Bay Company Archives, Provincial Archives of Manitoba.
191 (Upper) Hudson's Bay Company Archives, Provincial Archives of Manitoba. (Middle) Hudson's Bay Company Archives, Provincial Archives of Manitoba (53-78 N 6925/5380). (Lower) Hudson's Bay Company Archives, Provincial Archives of Manitoba (1981/39-492).
192 Hudson's Bay Company Archives, Provincial Archives of Manitoba (1987/363/M-67).
192–193 *Hudson's Bay* poster, 20th Century-Fox.
193 (Upper left) Hudson's Bay Company Archives, Provincial Archives of Manitoba (1987/363/M-67). (Upper right) Hudson's Bay Company Archives, Provincial Archives of Manitoba (1987/363/M-67). (Middle) Hudson's Bay Company Archives, Provincial Archives of Manitoba (1987/363/M-67). (Lower) Hudson's Bay Company Archives, Provincial Archives of Manitoba (1987/363/M-67).
194 Hudson's Bay Company Archives, Provincial Archives of Manitoba (1985/363/127).

195 National Archives of Canada (PA-143236).
197 Kevin Fleming.
198 Hudson's Bay Company.
199 Hudson's Bay Company.
200 Kevin Fleming.
201 (Upper) Hudson's Bay Company. (Lower) Provincial Archives of Alberta.
202 Hudson's Bay Company.
202–203 Provincial Archives of Alberta.
203 (Top left) Hudson's Bay Company. (Bottom left) Hudson's Bay Company. (Right) Hudson's Bay Company.
204 (Top) Hudson's Bay Company. (Middle) Zellers Inc.
204–205 Hudson's Bay Company
205 (Left) Hudson's Bay Company. (Right) Zellers Inc.
206–207 *Canoe in Fog* by Frances Ann Hopkins. Glenbow Museum (55.8.1).
209 *Albany Fort, North America.* Hudson's Bay Company Archives, Provincial Archives of Manitoba (B.3/d/102).
224 *Tracking the Rapids* by Frances Ann Hopkins. Royal Ontario Museum (952.168.2).
Back Flap Curtis Lantinga.

ACKNOWLEDGEMENTS

Many contributors made this work possible; among those especially deserving attention:

Thanks are primarily due to everyone at the Hudson's Bay Company Archives in Winnipeg, particularly **Shirlee Smith**, their Keeper, and **Debra Moore**, who, in her capacity as picture archivist, was of invaluable assistance in the preparation of this book.

At the National Archives of Canada, I must thank **Gloria MacKenzie** and, at the Canadian Government Photo Centre, **Jean-Marie Philippe**. Both helped speed various pictures and illustrations to the indefatigable **Ian R. Coutts** at Madison Press Books, who acted as photo editor. Others at Madison who assisted were **Marcy Laufer** and **Sandra Hall**, capably field-marshalled by the innovative and talented **Hugh Brewster**.

Pronk&Associates did an excellent job in the design and layout and in overseeing the countless details that went into page assembly.

A. Rolph Huband, Vice-President and Secretary of the Hudson's Bay Company, deserves thanks for the information he provided on the Hudson's Bay Company's recent history.

Pat Harding, my assistant at *Maclean's*, helped in a thousand ways. Finally, I must thank **Camilla Newman**, who read over this manuscript carefully and came up with many useful suggestions.

INDEX

Tracking the Rapids *by Frances Ann Hopkins*

DESIGN, ART DIRECTION
AND TYPOGRAPHY: Pronk&Associates

EDITORIAL: Hugh Brewster
Ian R. Coutts

EDITORIAL ASSISTANCE: Deborah Viets

PRODUCTION: Susan Barrable

PRODUCTION ASSISTANCE: Catherine A. Clark

COLOUR SEPARATION
AND PRINTING: Amilcare Pizzi, S.p.A.

BINDING: Legatoria del Verbano